the road AHEAD

the road AHEAD

Inspirational
Stories of
Open Hearts
& Minds

JANE SEYMOUR

A POST HILL PRESS BOOK

The Road Ahead:
Inspirational Stories of Open Hearts and Minds
© 2017 by Jane Seymour
All Rights Reserved
Represented by Licensing Matters Global, Inc.

ISBN: 978-1-68261-463-1
ISBN (eBook): 978-1-68261-464-8

Cover art by Tricia Principe, triciaprincipedesign.com

Cover photo by Charles Bush

Interior Design and Composition by Greg Johnson/Textbook Perfect

New media reinterpretation of photographs taken by Jane Seymour in Ibizia and Nova Scotia in 2017, exclusively for use in *The Road Ahead*, utilizing the advanced image processing software "Waterlogue" by Tinrocket, LLC.

Post Hill Press
New York • Nashville
posthillpress.com
Published in the United States of America

To my loving family who are always there for me.

To Cheri, Rachel, Susan, Mark, and my entire support team, thank you all for your loyalty and encouragement.

To David for all his loving and selfless support.

To the fans for your endless courage and inspiration.

To my mother, Mieke, who inspired us all to live with an Open Heart.

Contents

Part One
Surviving Illness and Other Challenges............. 1

Part Two
Families Come in Different Shapes and Sizes 43

Part Six
From Suffering to a Cause........................ 131

Part Seven
Self-Exploration and Survival 157

Acknowledgments

Paula Allen

Kim Campbell

Debra Englander

Sally Frankenberg

Annie Gould

David Green

Cheri Ingle

Greg Johnson

Susan Nagy Luks

Susan Madore

Mark Matheny

Jeff Palmer

Rachel Woods

Anthony Ziccardi and our friends
at Post Hill Press
To all the dedicated fans who have contributed
from around the world who continue to inspire me
by sharing their Open Heart journeys!

Foreword

I have always thought of myself as being very self-sufficient. When people would ask if they could help me do something, I'd say, "No thanks. I've got it." I felt like I had superhuman energy and that it took less time to do things myself than to explain what I wanted or needed to someone else. I thought I had everything under control and didn't really need anyone's help.

That mentality quickly changed when my husband Glen was diagnosed with Alzheimer's. I found myself becoming overwhelmed, exhausted, isolated, and depressed. I had no idea where the road ahead would lead, what kind of obstacles we might face, how long the journey would be, or if I had the strength to take it. I feared we could lose our friends, our freedom, and our future. I thought it was the end of the road for both of us, but Glen was the exact opposite.

Maybe it was the Alzheimer's that removed his fear and apprehension, but Glen simply seemed to have a pure and almost childlike excitement about living and enjoying life. He had an incredible sense of humor and was able to laugh at himself and find humor in every circumstance. When it came to facing almost any difficulty, he did it with confidence as if it was no big deal. If he saw a speed bump in the road, he would just go around it. I did my best to mirror his optimism because I didn't want him to be afraid. I knew that if he sensed my fear, it would bring him down with me, so I was determined to be strong for him.

Glen's producer, Julian Raymond, approached actress Jane Seymour and her then husband, filmmaker/actor James Keach (*Walk the Line*), and told them that Glen was getting ready to do a five-week tour to promote his new album after telling the world that he had just been diagnosed with Alzheimer's. Julian felt that Glen's courage and musicianship should be recorded for posterity before it was too late, and he implored Jane and James to consider having their company, PCH Films, document the tour.

Glen and I were already fans of Keach's filmmaking after seeing how he treated Johnny Cash's story with such dignity, respect, and sensitivity. We trusted him to do the same for us. Intrigued with the idea of a "rockumentary" about Glen's last tour under the shadow of Alzheimer's disease, James and his partner, Trevor Albert (*Groundhog Day*), watched every movie they could about Alzheimer's. Independent of each other, they both came to the same conclusion: they didn't feel that a movie about Alzheimer's could reach a wide audience. There was no hope, no cure, and no upside to the story. The subject matter was just too depressing. Despite this, they agreed to meet with us.

Julian set up a day for us to visit Jane and James at their Malibu estate. I've met a lot of celebrities in my lifetime, but for some reason I felt a little nervous to be meeting this power couple. I also felt nervous for Glen, considering that his illness and short-term memory loss made meeting new people a little challenging.

As we settled into their living room to chat, Jane reassured Glen and me that opening our hearts and letting people know what we were dealing with would give people permission to ask questions and offer help.

While we were talking, Jane's and James's teenaged son Johnny walked through the room carrying a guitar. Glen stopped him and said, "Hey, I play guitar. You want me to show you something?" Johnny said, "Sure," and handed Glen the guitar. Glen shredded an incredible solo as Johnny watched in awe. Glen handed the guitar back to him as if to say, "And that's how you do it, son." Johnny took the guitar back as if it had turned to gold through the Midas touch of Glen's fingers and retreated into his bedroom with a big smile on his face.

Glen spoke about his desire to educate and raise awareness about Alzheimer's and the need to find a cure. He was honest, sweet, loving, and very funny. He knew what he was up against and where the disease would ultimately take him, but he was not going to let it rob him of enjoying the present. He wanted to continue living his life, doing what he loved with the people he loved.

It wasn't long before Johnny walked through the room again with the same guitar in hand. Once more, Glen said, "Hey, I play guitar. You want me to show you something?" "Sure?" said Johnny, somewhat perplexed, as he handed Glen the guitar for the second time. Glen shredded yet another incredible solo and handed the guitar back to Johnny.

Everyone was amazed as Alzheimer's manifested itself right before their eyes. Glen's short-term memory was clearly failing, but his musical memory was fully intact.

After meeting Glen and the rest of our family, James and Jane told us that the way they viewed Alzheimer's had changed dramatically. They began to imagine a documentary very different from any other film on the topic. Glen's positive energy, optimism, courage, sense of humor, and determination had inspired them, and they decided they wanted to tell his story.

When Glen publicly announced he had Alzheimer's, we received an outpouring of love and encouragement unlike anything we could have imagined! Every show was completely sold out and offers to do more shows kept pouring in. What started out as a five-week tour turned into almost two years and 151 sold-out performances.

Taking care of Glen on the road was very challenging, to say the least. I quickly learned there was no way I could handle everything by myself. When someone would ask if they could help, I opened my heart and said, "Yes!" The more I said yes, the more love I experienced, and the more friends I made.

None of us truly knows what lies ahead on the road before us, but I have learned that living with an open heart means you don't have to walk the road alone. As one of the 15 million caregivers caring for a loved one with dementia, I know how much we need one another's support, encouragement, and inspiration.

The road ahead for me is paved with purpose. I have made it my mission to improve the quality of life for people with dementia and their caregivers by launching CareLiving.org, a website designed to inspire, encourage, and empower caregivers to care for themselves while caring for others. With a host of guest writers, specialists, musicians, doctors, and other caregivers, CareLiving is poised to become the go-to source of hope and progress for caregivers worldwide by raising awareness through social media, events, education, and real-world actions.

The Road Ahead is a collection of essays by people who have blazed a trail through trials, hurdled over challenges, navigated through treacherous circumstances, and turned adversity into advocacy in order to help others. Their examples shine like a light to make the journey safer and easier for those walking in their footsteps.

Kim Campbell

Kim Campbell was the wife of country and pop music star Glen Campbell and founder of CareLiving.org. She and Glen were married for 34 years; he died in August 2017. Their three children—Cal, Shannon, and Ashley—are all musicians following in their father's footsteps.

Introduction

Life is full of changes, some expected and many more unexpected. You're likely to struggle as you adjust to change, especially if it is unexpected and big. Whether it is something mundane, such as starting a new job or a new school, or a more significant event, such as illness, divorce, or even the loss of a loved one, you must find a way to reset. It may take time and there will be days when you want to stay under the covers and hide but eventually, you will get up and start again.

Looking back and asking, "why me?" gets tiresome quickly—for you and the people around you. I simply won't ask this question nor should you! You must let go and get past whatever has happened or is bothering you and instead say, "Now I will do...." Looking at your road ahead is much more empowering than making excuses or hanging onto feelings about something that occurred when you were a child. No one ever said life would be perfect so when things change, you need to be open-minded and open-hearted and embrace the "new" future.

From my work with the Open Hearts Foundation, in partnership with Kay Jewelers, I have met and spoken with hundreds of people who have overcome difficult situations and, in fact, turned their hardships into ways to help others and make positive changes in the world. Each year the Open Hearts Foundation recognizes achievements in various areas including health, education, arts, and sports, from many, many worthy applicants.

This book features essays from some people who have been recognized by the Open Hearts Foundation, along with many others who exemplify its message of finding ways to prevail over illness or adversity, not just for themselves, but as a way to support and comfort others. For example, Andrea Rizzo lost her only daughter in a drunk-driving accident, but ended up fulfilling her daughter's dream by starting a foundation of providing dance therapy to schools and hospitals. Jesse Billauer was a champion surfer until he became paralyzed. Not only did Jesse go on to invent equipment that allows paralyzed people to go surfing, he continues to surf and travels around the world, encouraging others who face physical challenges. Lori Ames gave up her job at a high-powered book publicity company after her son Robert was diagnosed with a brain tumor. She started her own publicity firm to allow her more flexibility during her son's treatment and now does work for the Children's Brain Tumor Foundation and The Michael Magro Foundation, two organizations that helped her son in his recovery. Mary Ann Marino was born with spina bifida, endured years of pain and hospitalization, and later had a leg amputated. But she explains, "If I've learned one thing above all it's that reaching out to others, whether for help or to offer your own help, is the only way to begin to answer the question—why me?"

Introduction

The difficulties faced by the contributors in *The Road Ahead* include destructive and abusive relationships, serious illnesses, loss of loved ones, and more. As you read these essays, you'll learn that the authors accomplished far more than they could ever have imagined if their lives hadn't suddenly changed. When you remain on one path for your whole life, you can't grow. Many of us are afraid of change but only by facing unexpected challenges and interacting with other people can you continue to grow and experience positive and wonderful adventures.

My mother was in a Japanese internment camp during World War II and her attitude had a tremendous influence on me. Despite unbelievable suffering and sorrow, she maintained a positive outlook. While in the camp and throughout her life, she tried to assist people who were worse off than she was. She taught me to live in the moment and connect with people and offer to help them.

Think out of the box. If you care about someone, you can help. You can work to organize a nonprofit. You can write, paint, or create something. You have to learn to express yourself in a way that allows you to be happy in your own skin and also have a purpose. I'm an actress and an artist; I don't know what your gift is. Think about what you can share with the world that is unique to you. Everything is fluid. The world moves, your health moves, your relationships move; we aren't meant to be still. You can learn to adapt and use change to your advantage. You can find joy, purpose, compassion, and empathy—the essential emotions of the human experience.

There is no perfect way to act. You should be authentic. Be the real you. Be your own best! If you try to do your best, you will feel good about yourself. Stop saying, "I could have done better." Instead, ask what you can learn from this experience to be better in the future. Smile. Do your best. Cheer on others. And just like the open heart symbol of giving and receiving, if you can love and feel good about yourself, then you will love others and in turn, find purpose for your life.

I hope you find inspiration in these people and their stories. I know that they have inspired me.

Jane Seymour

Part One

Surviving Illness and Facing Challenges

None of us knows when we or someone we love will be diagnosed with a major illness or be severely injured in an accident. Life is completely unpredictable and people don't know how they will cope or adjust when they face the unexpected. It is hard to imagine the "new" journey but these stories share a common theme. They show that accepting and never giving up is the definition of a life well lived. Happiness gained by helping others gives us purpose. Purpose gives up hope and love. Living in the moment and appreciating what we have, indeed counting our blessings is key.

Follow Your Dreams

I was an athletic kid and by the time I was age seventeen, I was a top 100 surfer. I knew I wanted to be a professional surfer and I was looking forward to the future. But everything changed on March 25, 1996. It was a beautiful morning and I went surfing just like I did most mornings. Usually, I went by myself but on this day, I was with friends. A wave knocked me back and I hit a sandbar. I couldn't get up and I was lying face down in the water. I called my friends for help but they thought I was just goofing around. Finally, when my best friend came over, I told him he had to keep my head out of the water because I was really hurt and I was going to drown.

I was carried out of the water and a lifeguard put a neck brace on me; I was taken by helicopter to the hospital. The next thing I knew I was strapped into a contraption with tubes in and out of my body. I had a severe spinal cord injury, and I was a quadriplegic.

It was tough at first. I was used to doing whatever I wanted and traveling around the world. Suddenly, I was dependent on others 24/7. I had a choice: I could stay in my wheelchair and feel sorry for myself. Or I could take a more optimistic view and do what I wanted to do with my life. Initially, I was sad and spent some time wondering why this happened to me. I thought that bad things happen to bad people, not someone like me. But somehow, I knew that I had to slow down and think about my life. I almost dropped out of high school but the principal was very supportive and I graduated with my friends. I still think about where I would be if I were still walking. But I can't dwell on what I can't do. I have to focus on what I can do.

I knew that I wanted to get back to surfing. It took about three years because I had to find the right equipment and tools, because no one was helping disabled people surf back then. But once I got back into the water, I thought how good I felt and I knew that I wanted to give this feeling to other people.

That was the beginning of Life Rolls On, but I didn't know that the organization would grow to where it is today. At first, we held one event and that led to more and more events around the country. Now we have about 100 people with various disabilities and 300 volunteers participating at every event. It just grew on its own. We built up a big volunteer base, which makes it a lot easier. We find sponsors to underwrite the events. It's important to find sponsors that will commit to multi-year sponsorships so that the events will be ongoing. I wouldn't want to hold a one-time-only event. We can't grow too fast. We don't have a huge infrastructure and we need to find the right people who are dedicated to the activities. I've given our playbook to people overseas so they can start similar programs. It wouldn't be fair for them to have to wait for Life Rolls On. Maybe at some point, we'll partner with them.

Having an injury like mine is an emotional roller coaster, both for the patient and his or her family. I give speeches and I also talk to newly injured people at rehab hospitals. There are many more opportunities now than when I had my accident twenty-one years ago. I know these patients are lost and scared; if I give them a little bit of hope, that's great. I am grateful for the people who visited me in the hospital and gave me hope.

In some ways, the wheelchair makes it easier for me. It is a visible sign of my injury and opens doors because people will ask me how they can help. But there are many people who are suffering whose problems aren't obvious but they can still use your help. When you volunteer, you'll meet all sorts of people and these experiences can change your life.

The most important message I have for anyone coping with an illness or disability is to follow your own dreams, not those of your friends or parents. You should always have something to look forward to or you'll always be stuck in the same place. If you follow your heart and your mind, you can accomplish whatever you want. Figure out what you're passionate about and then everything else will fall in place.

—**Jesse Billauer**, World Champion Quadriplegic Surfer
and Life Rolls On Founder & Executive Director/CEO,
liferollson.org

Don't Take a Single Second for Granted

My name is Krystal and in 2002, at the age of twenty-two, I survived a twenty-six-hour brain surgery at The Ohio State University Hospital. After going through such a challenge, I have learned not to take a single second for granted. I have learned to keep a balance in my life and to inspire others to do the same. I developed my own website to share my story, my affiliation with the American Brain Tumor Association, and to offer support and awareness to others. This year, 2017, will mark fifteen years of being a survivor!

—**Krystal Patterson**

Making a Difference with My Difference

Born with a purple port wine stain birthmark that covers half of my face, I've always known what it means to stand out. Growing up, I had to quickly get accustomed to people constantly making comments about my appearance and staring my way. My mom often tried to block me from seeing strangers whose gazes lingered longer than they ought to. Yet, at the age of five, when she couldn't block a stranger's stare, I remember her telling me, "I know what they're doing is rude and unkind. But, what if they're having one of the worst days of their life and you smile at them? Maybe you'll be the only one to smile at them today, and maybe you'll make a friend." Her response in that situation prepared me for a lifetime of people staring and making comments. This moment helped me prepare for many situations that would come in the future.

Three years ago, someone stole my image on Facebook and turned me into an unkind meme. I was turned into an internet, nameless, spotlight attraction—which went viral to over 30 million people around the world. They say a picture is worth a thousand words, yet thousands of strangers were adding their fictional thousands of words next to my image. There were thousands of comments, and I found myself reading over 30,000 of them. Strangers around the world came together in unison, agreeing that my beauty was nonexistent, and that I'd, "better meet a plastic surgeon soon who can fix that."

Processing all that I saw and read, for the first time in my life, I realized how different I must look compared to the majority of society and how misunderstood my condition is.

For the first time in my life, I saw myself through the eyes of thousands of strangers, questioning my appearance.

After this happened, I initially had some incredibly dark days. My confidence was depleted, and for every single day for the last three years, I haven't forgotten that I look different and I haven't forgotten my unique appearance.

Thankfully, I have had amazing friends who support me. Several weeks after going viral, one friend called me with concern. She knew I was struggling, that I was in a dark place. She knew that my struggle, emotions, and the process of healing mattered and were valid—but she also knew the importance of keeping me accountable, reminding me of who I was in the moments I forgot. Talking on the phone, she reminded me that I had a choice, "At this point you need to decide which Crystal you're going to be. Are you going to be the 'overcomer Crystal,' or the 'self-pity Crystal?' Either is fine, and you get to choose. But as a friend, I need to know so I can better support you." In that moment, my friend couldn't turn the light on for me, but she did help me remember which wall the light switch was on and that I had the power to change my scenery by the flip of a switch.

Yet, while I've only been able to see one puzzle piece at time during this journey, I also know that God can see the whole puzzle. There is more than I can see. There is a bigger picture. In that moment, I can use my story to help others. After my friend called me, I created a "God-sized dream board" to help me focus on the big picture of life ahead of me, but also to remember that God had hope and a plan for my future; my story wasn't over just yet.

Now I do public speaking in schools, churches, youth groups, and hospitals. I recently spoke to students in Taiwan. I keep busy with my writing; I've completed several children's books. While there hasn't been a day since going viral when I haven't forgotten the purple hue on my face, I choose to let this empower me—knowing that I can keep making a difference with my difference.

As a speaker and writer, I often hear from other people with similar birthmarks. I've heard from women who were put in makeup by the age of two by their own mothers, and women who are forced to wear makeup to bed because their husbands don't want to wake up to "see that." Many people write to me—birthmark or not—sharing that they wish they had the courage to also share their stories, but that they don't have a voice. But that's where they're wrong.

It took me nearly twenty years and my photo going viral to realize I had a voice. But here's the thing—we have the power to stick up for what is right; we have the power to stick up for others and more importantly, for ourselves.

We all have a voice, but we often forget that not every voice is the same. What you have to say, however you want to say it, is important. Use your words. Speak them, write them, blog them, YouTube them, put them to a melodious tune. Create that piece of art, shoot that photo series. Whatever way you communicate best—do it. What you have to say is important, and people will listen. Write that book, sing that song. You have a story to tell.

—**Crystal Hodges**, crystalhodges.com

Giving from the Heart Gives to the Soul

I have a rare disease called transverse myelitis that has left me bedbound most days. I need a wheelchair to get around but I cannot let this crippling disease stop me from helping others. Each and every day I reach out on several social media sites to assist those in need, whether it is to help a homeless family to find furniture and clothes for their new home or to collect and distribute items for my annual food pantry. Every day of the year I fulfill needs that others have, and I am the owner/administrator of Hometown Heroes, my local charity. Just because my body is slowly becoming paralyzed doesn't mean I don't have a purpose, and my purpose is to help others each and every single day, anyway I possibly can. If I can't find the way, I find the right people who can. Giving from the heart gives to the soul.

—Anonymous

Take the Next Step

Life changed unexpectedly for us on a cold, snowy day in January 1986. Dan, the love of my life and the father of our three children, was hit by an out-of-control car on a snowy canyon road. Suddenly, in an instant, life changed. This wasn't the, "Oh, I am having a bad day" kind of bump in the road. This was, "My life train just derailed!" leaving in its wake a scene of carnage and pain. The track that I was on ended at that moment and I was forced to create a new path for our life journey. I had to pull the pieces from the wreckage that could be salvaged and move on. I wasn't even sure what the next few hours would look like, let alone a new life path. Somewhere deep inside, I found the strength to take the next step, and started to assemble a new life track from the figurative pieces of twisted metal and glass shards.

Yes, it was painful. There were buckets of tears and a cargo full of fear that slowed me on the path to my new destination, but I knew I had to keep going. Even if I couldn't see the end result, I had faith that God would take care of me if I continued to press forward. I wanted nothing more than to have Dan wake up from his coma, and walk out of the hospital back to the life that we had known. But that was not to be. God had a different plan for us, a plan that would cause us to stretch and to grow along the way. God knows our abilities more than we know ourselves, and we just needed to move forward, trusting in Him even though the end result was not in sight. I was blessed as I trusted God and watched His miracle unfold. First, Dan opened his eyes, and then he started to perspire and was able to maintain his own body temperature. He was completely paralyzed, but we watched as he started to move the left side of his body, and then the right. Slowly and surely he progressed until he was off life support, able to breathe on his own. After several months, he could even walk with assistance!

Probably the most amazing miracle was that Dan's soul was still intact. Even though speech was difficult due to paralysis of his lips and vocal chords, we found new ways to communicate. The emotional bond and love that we shared between us was still there. I watched this giant soul of a man face the physical limitations that he had with a smile on his face, and I loved him even more.

What do you do when life slaps you up the side of the head? How do you move on? The faith of my youth held steady through these dark hours and my connection to God deepened and prepared me for the years ahead.

In addition, our network of family and friends provided a support system that helped see us through. An accident of this magnitude doesn't just happen to an individual, it happens to a family and a community. I learned that there is much goodness in this world as others came to our aid. It didn't stop after the accident either, but has continued over the years, by those closest to us and even from strangers. Each act of kindness lifted our burden and helped us take the next step forward. Never underestimate the power of a simple act of kindness and the ability it has to provide hope and encouragement to the receiver. We have been the receiver of such and can attest to the strengthening power of a seemingly small act.

The most important thing I learned was to move on. What has happened is in the past, and we must look to the future to find our way. As I came to accept the fact that my life would be different, I began to have the power to move forward on our new life track. The key was to *move*...to keep trudging along putting the pieces together as part of the journey. Life is messy. Accepting that it is messy allowed me the freedom to move, knowing that I would make mistakes along the way, but knowing that I would get part of it right too.

It is in the journey that we gather our strength. Even though our life hopes and dreams were crushed in a moment, from the rubble came new hopes and new dreams. As the hope of walking dream faded, the hope of biking came alive. After many failed attempts and years of trying, we found a way to make this dream a reality. Dan not only bikes for his own freedom and mobility, he is able to bike for others too. This past year, he finished a 100-mile ride to raise money for cancer research.

The message for your life challenges is please just don't give up! Keep moving forward. It may be a blur and you can't see the end in sight, but as you keep going, you will find your new life track has some pretty stunning views on the way. Life can be amazing, but we have to keep pressing forward to find the joy that awaits us on the other side of hard.

—**LaNae Maughan**, author of a forthcoming memoir
with her husband Dan, smileyourwaythru.com

Nothing Will Deter Me

I have dedicated my life to making a difference in the world. In 2010, I went deep into DRC-Congo to share the story on why women and children are being horrifically raped. I stayed out there trusting someone in dangerous circumstances and came back and lost my home. I was homeless for seventeen months but came out with a vision to help empower women even further, which I am doing to this day. All adversities in my life, including abuse, will not deter me from doing good work to help others.

—**Tess Cacciatore**

Making Someone Smile

I'm a survivor of a lifetime of abuse. My greatest asset is my open heart and willingness to be mindful of others' struggles. Nothing came easy. It hasn't changed; it hasn't been easy being me. I work daily to become a better person, a person who can make you smile and someone who sees and hears you. My greatest reward comes from knowing I've made a difference in your day. This is my purpose for living. Often alone I struggle to live, to be seen, to be heard. I know the pain that comes with that life.

—**Rebecca Mitchell**

Facing Struggles with Grace

Everything happens for a reason. Right? The problem is when you're eight years old, that doesn't bring much comfort when you are literally staring through a fence watching the neighborhood kids playing board games in someone's clubhouse, or standing alone after everyone else has been picked for a scrub team, or watching longingly as everyone heads off on their bikes without you on a hot summer day. I was born with spina bifida, which is a small opening in the spine that usually results in devastating disabilities and, often, early death. My parents were told that I had the mildest case the doctors had ever seen. The disease only affected my balance and some nerve sensation in my legs and feet. It kept me from many of the normal activities that kids engaged in, and as a result I was frequently alienated from my peers, but I had actually been quite lucky (or so we thought). But as a child, I didn't feel lucky. I just kept wondering, why me?

In high school, an innocent trip to the beach resulted in a tiny puncture wound—because of my lack of nerve sensation—that would change my life. The puncture grew into an ulcer, which could only be treated by complete bed rest. I would attend school each year for a few months and then around October the infection would resurface; it would be time to clean out my desk and I would then remain in bed for the next nine months or so. It wasn't easy in my early teens living life from the sidelines, but I tried to use my time as best I could between studying on my own (along with the help of a lovely tutor), teaching myself to draw and play the guitar (albeit badly), and even to type. Finally, in my senior year, the infection seemed to subside but God had something far more devastating in store.

- Just as I was entering college, my mother was diagnosed with breast cancer. College is supposed to be a time of wonder and exploration but my college years were spent watching my mother deal with the ravages of this cruel disease while I again was left wondering "why." I couldn't do anything about the cancer, but I needed to do something for her so I learned to cook. I studied cookbooks from the library and experimented with different dishes and presented them as my gift. It was the only way I could think of to brighten her days and the only thing I could control.

After her death, I continued with my studies and eventually graduated from college, thinking about a career in early education. Before I could pursue that path, however, I decided to visit an orthopedic surgeon to see if my gait could be surgically corrected. Little did I know that this doctor's appointment would lead to my most difficult challenge of all. After the doctor examined me, he said that the ulcer I had been dealing with since my teens had developed into a full- fledged bone infection that had literally eaten away much of the bone in my foot. What followed was a course of six weeks of IV treatment every three months for the next decade. When the hospital stays became more and more frequent, limited surgical options were tried including amputation of a few toes, then half my foot. Finally, I was informed that the ultimate permanent solution was a full amputation of my leg from the knee down. Without it I would never be able to work full-time, lead a normal life free of the pain and constant fever I was living with, and in fact, I might die. At this point, death seemed like a viable option as did just doing nothing and letting nature take its course. But deep inside, I know that I'm a survivor and that deep belief, combined with a strong faith instilled in me by my parents from childhood, finally helped me to make the hardest decision of my life. I agreed to the surgery.

If everything happens for a reason why did I have to lose my leg? Was it to show me that I would always have the strength to be able to overcome whatever I would be asked to deal with in the future? When I finally decided to have the amputation, I felt the most incredible sense of peace I had ever felt. I hadn't been able to control the infection that had robbed me of so many years of my life but I would now take control over my future.

When people hear my story, they often ask how I've dealt with so much loss. My instinct is to simply say, "You do what you have to do at the time; it's not really a conscious choice." But I have noticed that when faced with an obstacle I usually approach it from several directions. First, I try to assess the situation. Okay, this has happened, now what can I do to deal with it. How much of this can I control? Second, I let it go and trust that whatever I decide, God will make something good come of it if I step back and let Him. I then ask for His help in dealing with the situation with as much grace as possible. And finally, I reach out to others, a choice that often has not only strengthened bonds, but has led to some of the most incredible friendships of my life. I believe we are given challenges sometimes to transform us but also, on occasion, to effect a transformation in others.

When I was in the hospital for my amputation, an elderly Italian woman was there at the same time. She was the matriarch of the family and she was always looking out for everyone else. She was dealing with a much more overwhelming loss than I was. She had just lost both her legs and felt that now she would no longer be of use to anyone. She refused therapy and was waiting to die. A therapist had told me about her and said that this woman had been quietly watching me every day in the gym as I struggled to regain my own ability to walk. She had apparently been so impressed by how hard I was working that she was inspired to go back into therapy and try to do the best she could to overcome her own challenge.

Since my surgery I've lost a dear friend to cancer and her mother as well, and a few years ago I went through five months of rehab after being hit by a car on my way home from work. Whenever I feel like it's all too much, I think of everyone—strangers and friends—whose lives have been devastated by illness and unbearable loss. Watching their struggles has affected my own and made me more determined than ever to try to face whatever comes with the grace I've seen each of them exhibit every day. Is it always easy? Of course not, but none of us faces our struggles alone. If I've learned one thing above all it's that reaching out to others, whether for help or to offer your own help, is the only way to begin to answer the question: why me?

—**Mary Ann Marino**

Running to Help Others

I've been running for a long time. I enjoy it, and I've met a lot of great people because of it. I started running for Fred's team, named for Fred Lebow, the co-founder of the New York City Marathon.

Since 2002, I have completed more than 200 road races, including twenty-two marathons. And I have raised over 125,000 dollars to find cures for lung, pancreatic, and pediatric cancers. Now when I run, I'm raising money for Memorial Sloan Kettering to fight cancer. It's become personal for me since my father died of pancreatic cancer three years ago.

I'm always going to be a runner so raising money through an activity I'm already doing is easy. Now there are many organized events and programs to raise money from running, cycling, and other events. Why not help scientists and doctors find a cure for terrible diseases?

—Jeffrey Kamberg

One Path Ends and Another Begins

When I was diagnosed with MS I thought my life was over because I couldn't work as a teacher anymore. Eventually I found out that if I looked out for others I could still do a lot of things, like keeping the library in our small town alive. I still open it twice a week (as a volunteer). I helped found an association (and now I'm the head of it) that organizes events for the children and seniors in our area. I think I'm more active now than ever—because I kept my heart open.

—Marion Goetz

Surviving Abuse

My memoir, *Driving in the Dark,* chronicles how I survived childhood abuse and ended up being adopted at age eighteen.

I've been married for forty-two years to my college sweetheart, and I am an advocate for the adoption of older children.

My mother was an alcoholic, a barbiturates addict, and she also had emotional problems. She was married seven times; in fact, I had to find out my legal birth name when I was about thirteen. I ending up getting into trouble and was put in foster care three times: at ages nine, eleven, and finally at age thirteen when I asked a school counselor for help. That last plea for help led to a several months-long court battle, and I was sent to a foster family. This family later became my permanent family and their love saved me.

When I was age eleven, my mother had a seizure, and I had to drive a '52 Buick out of the mountains to get help for her. It was a very traumatic time and this experience taught me:

In order to survive, I had to grab the wheel and be proactive. If my mother had been driving, we both could have been killed.

When I was driving I was terrified but I was certain that I wouldn't run anyone over. I followed the white line just as I followed my belief in a higher power. I wouldn't stop and just kept going.

Take crisis as opportunity. I had the courage to change; I saw what was normal around me and I knew what I wanted to be.

After I lost four jobs in rapid succession, I knew that my clinical depression and memory issues needed to be addressed. I spent two years writing my memoir with an incredible amount of support from my adoptive family. Then I sat on the book for seven years. Finally, after my adoptive father died at age ninety-nine, I said I would complete the book.

I worked with an incredible editor and published the book, which really was a love letter to my adoptive family. It also shows the love I have for my wounded biological mother. Writing the book freed me incredibly. Suddenly, I could remember things and I was able to resurrect my stunted theatrical career. I'm now writing a one-woman show.

When I talk to people, they are incredibly supportive. They believe in my experience and want to share my courage, resilience, and tenacity. One day a woman told me, "I have never told a soul but I was abused until I left my home to get married...but when I see the calmness and joy in you, I know that today I will tell my husband and my family what happened so I can get beyond that."

You come forward when you hit bottom, when it's them or you. I knew I wouldn't have survived if I stayed with my mother. I didn't want to get beaten or worse. It was either her or me.

—**Zoe Niklas**

My Heart Is Open to Everyone

When I was twenty I was in an accident and had to have my leg amputated above the knee. I was determined not to feel sorry for myself. I returned to work and met my future husband. I have three sons, five grandkids, and am very active. I have had other challenges. There is alcoholism in my family, and my youngest son has had two kidney transplants. I keep my heart open to everyone knowing many suffer without complaint. I live a day at a time. I still hate having to put on an artificial leg every day but, oh well. My heart is open to everyone.

—**Johnnie Lahatte**

A Lifetime of Self-Healing

As a child and young adult, I endured different kinds of physical/sexual/emotional abuse, and I trudged my way through PTSD. My childhood consisted of pretty pictures and pretty smiles and happy times with some dark undercurrents. Each event threatened to keep me down. Yet, once I saw the light at the end of the tunnel of every tough situation that I've fought my way through, I immediately knew that I would be able to channel the event in a positive direction. By the time I was nine years old I knew I was going into the mental health profession. I found inspiration with Rainbow Days Inc. in Dallas, Texas. By helping to lead their support groups for homeless children, I was reminded of strength, hope, and healing. The children awed me with their resilience and bright spirits. It was empowering to lift others. I am forever grateful for that spark that has inspired a lifetime of self-healing and helping others through my own career of therapy, service, and charity.

—**Anonymous**

Spreading Awareness and Hope

I was born with a congenital heart defect (CHD). At that time, there was very little awareness of such birth defects. My mother, Anna Jaworski, set out to change this, and started Baby Hearts Press, a business publishing books to help families of children with heart defects. She went on to found a charity called Hearts Unite the Globe, which provides information about heart defects and sponsors a weekly radio show called *Heart to Heart with Anna*, where they discuss important issues in the CHD community. My story has been shared through the books that Baby Hearts Press publishes, and I have been interviewed on the radio show several times. I have been able to spread hope to families with sick children by letting them know that the future can still be a bright one. Hearts Unite the Globe is still a young charity, but they have already reached and helped many people.

—Alex Jaworski

There Is Still So Much to Do

On September 15, 2012, I underwent stage 3 colorectal surgery. That, for me, was a journey that started me down a road of understanding how many of all ages are affected by this disease. Cancer is not a death sentence, and for me it opened up a way to help others in life. I crochet or knit breast prosthesis for cancer survivors and help others in any way I can. It has been five years cancer-free now for me, and I stay positive. There is still so much to do in my life.

—Brenda Powell

Painting Has Saved My Life

I was in a car accident and suffered a brain injury. It changed everything about my life. I taught myself to oil paint so I could find a diversion from my struggles while trying to rebuild my life. I had no way to make an income. I began selling my paintings about the story of the redheaded woman. I challenge myself to paint all subjects and sell them all over the country. I also donate paintings to raise money to help others with their struggles. Painting has saved my life.

—**Pamela Johnson**

I Won't Quit My Fight

I am forty-three. I have cerebral palsy and progressive spastic paraplegia, which is slowly taking the use of my legs. Still I have written and self-published thirty-four books. I won't quit my fight.

—**Jennifer Anderson**

Asking for Help Is a Sign of Strength

Things were dark in January 2008. I was taking two hormones, a steroid, an anti-asthma medication, and fifty herbal and vitamin pills. I had recently finished six months of high-dose antibiotic therapy and had tried almost every alternative healing approach and healing diet in the known universe. Two doctors said that I had chronic Lyme disease. Others said I had Chronic Fatigue Syndrome. Another diagnosed me with "an unknown autoimmune disorder." All I knew was that I had a chronic cough, body aches, vertigo, and fatigue so intense that some days I couldn't make a fist. I cancelled lunch with friends for my thirty-ninth birthday because sitting up and socializing was more than I could manage. I had felt that way for almost six years.

Fast forward to one year later, January 2009, when I threw a party for my fortieth birthday and danced all night. No longer on any medications, I was running regularly and was finally back to work. After six years spent mainly in bed or doctors' offices, all this "normal" activity felt like a gift.

How did I get from 2008 to 2009? By overcoming my resistance and asking for help to find and follow my unique path to health.

Let me explain. In the first year of my illness, I was told to try a "raw foods diet," which meant eating only raw vegetables, sprouts, nuts, and seeds. My response was essentially, "You're crazy. Who does that?"

Over the years, as treatment after treatment failed, I kept encountering people who had recovered from symptoms similar to mine using that raw diet. The theory, simply put, is that eating only raw, organic vegetables gives the body the enzymes and nutrients that the immune system needs to beat back whatever challenge is thrown at it.

However, I didn't consider that to be a viable option. On top of its pseudo-science, far-out nature, it seemed impossible to follow. I was a sick mom with two lively preschool boys. I didn't have the time or energy to grow sprouts, juice greens, and make a whole set of raw meals for myself while feeding my sons. So, even though I eventually came to think it might not be a bad idea, I didn't even consider it.

I also never considered asking for help to try the diet. In fact, I had resisted getting any help during my entire illness. In hindsight, I see that I was afraid that if I was the one being supported, instead of the one supporting others, those others might not love or respect me as much. In addition, my parents, with all the best intentions, had raised me to believe that it was way better to give than to receive, and that health matters were private. Everything changed when I noticed that those beliefs were no longer serving me.

There are so many ways that I did *not* accept support in the early years of my illness: I did not accept friends' offers to do food shopping, or the generous offers of my parents and parents-in-law to pay for help around the house. I also did not ask people to accompany me to medical appointments, cook for my family, or review treatment options with me.

I spent hours and hours alone, exhausted, scared, and confused, searching for a cure and working with my husband to hold our family together without enough support, all because I couldn't ask for it. Doing everything by myself just made me sicker. That was a big mistake.

That finally changed in January 2008, when, feeling I had run out of options and with the encouragement of my husband, David, I began to explain my health challenge to more people and ask for and accept help. That extra support, in turn, enabled me to do the hard work of taking on that raw vegan diet for almost two years. It made a difference almost immediately. To this day, I eat a mainly vegan diet with lots of raw veggies, and occasional cheats. If I cheat too much, however; my old symptoms begin to creep back. David says I'm like a Formula One race car—I take only high-octane fuel.

In today's society, where the highest compliment is being called "self-made," we often regard accepting help as a sign of weakness. I would still be sick if I had bought into that message.

Having a wide variety of support to achieve important goals is not a sign of weakness. It's a sign of strength—of leadership. When you take that leadership and reach out to your friends and family for support, you may think that you are burdening them, but when done thoughtfully, with room to say no, you are actually offering them three precious gifts:

First, they get to deepen their relationship with you by joining in this effort.

Second, to be intimately involved in another person's journey as he or she steers in a new direction is a priceless opportunity. Whether they learn how to make a better salad, gain new insights into acceptance and perseverance, or discover how to handle a medical appointment productively, your friends and family will grow from the experience with you.

Third, supporting you often directly benefits your friends and family. If you invite a friend to join you at the gym twice per week, you are not imposing; you are offering her a hand.

If you are sick, your loved ones may have watched you struggle for months or even years with little sense of how to help. By giving them specific instructions on how they can support you, you are presenting them with a gift that many (but not all) of them have been waiting for. They don't have to sit by and feel helpless. They can do something!

My friends and family were so impacted by my dramatic healing that they began sending their sick friends and family to me for help. Eventually, I quit my day job and wrote a book and began providing coaching and workshops to share not the raw foods diet, but the skills to find your unique path to health and how to stick to it.

The most important skills include the ability to be vulnerable, admit how hard it may be to achieve your health goal, and ask for help—in a proactive, thoughtful way that brings others along with you to greater health.

Whether they are battling cancer, diabetes, chronic pain, or another health challenge, I have seen countless people change their lives when they take the risk to admit their struggles and ask for help.

If you are facing a health challenge and haven't been able to ask for support, imagine if the tables were turned and a close friend or family member were suddenly ill, wouldn't you want him or her to ask you for support and give you clear instructions on what to do? If you can't ask for help for you, do it for your loved ones. They are waiting for you.

—**Janette Hillis-Jaffe**, author of *Everyday Healing:*
Stand Up, Take Charge, and Get Your Health Back…
One Day at a Time

Finish Your Race

I was diagnosed with acute myeloid leukemia (AML), a potentially fatal blood cancer, on September 14, 2005. With this diagnosis came a sense of urgency I could feel. I saw it in the nurses' faces and heard it in the doctors' voices. And I was receiving far too much attention and wasn't quite sure why! It didn't take me long to understand the *why*! I had a twenty-five to thirty percent chance of surviving this type of cancer. So, the race was on! I endured five rounds of chemo, culminating in a successful stem cell transplant on May 12, 2006. This became my new "birthday"! A birthday I celebrate every year with great fanfare. This date marks the day I became a "survivor." But that was simply one day in what became an even longer and more significant journey.

There were notable moments in my journey (race) from the first round of chemo to the stem cell transplant, all of which tested my physical, emotional, mental, and spiritual strength over eight months. Almost from the first day of my treatment I chose to look at AML as something I would fight and beat, primarily because this is how I always approach problems in my life. My approach was no different in my cancer journey as I was always looking and thinking forward.

Battling cancer was an eye opener and taught me a great deal about myself and life in general. It's incredible how your perspective can change when you learn your life may suddenly come to an end. With my life in the balance, I took a closer look at who I was, what motivated me, and what was important to me. I wasn't always happy or pleased with the discoveries I made. I was successful in business and had put financial success above the most important relationships in my life. As a result, I had missed so much that life had to offer.

Cancer changed my perspective. Work is still important to me; however, I approach it so much differently. I wouldn't tell you to stop working or doing something you are passionate about, however I would tell you to add something to your life that will make it more satisfying and impactful to the people around you. I am (now) committed to making a difference in other people's lives.

My journey (race) with cancer was filled with uncertainty and challenges on a day-by-day basis. Fortunately, my journey (race) was also filled with victories that led to invaluable life lessons and strategies that have changed my life. As an example, I discovered that adversity affects us all, but it doesn't define us—it's the way we react that determines and changes the outcome.

It's been almost eleven years since I was diagnosed with leukemia and from the potential tragedy of my diagnosis I am giving my all to make a difference in the world. I have chosen to give back and in the process, I've accomplished things I never dreamed were possible. I devote as much time as possible raising dollars (and awareness) for blood cancer research. I also share my experience with cancer to cancer patients and survivors whenever I have the opportunity.

I have raised thousands of dollars for the Leukemia & Lymphoma Society (LLS). I am an outspoken advocate for the organization and a member of the North Texas Board of Trustees. I am a marathon coach for Team in Training (TNT) and have completed 18 marathons in the U.S. and internationally, raising over $100,000 for the organization. I co-founded a nonprofit race, The Honored Hero Run (Honored Hero is the title LLS gives to blood cancer survivors). This race donates its net proceeds for blood cancer research and has raised more than $140,000 for LLS in eight years.

Everyone will face some type of setback in life, whether it is illness, job loss, bankruptcy, the loss of a loved one, a marital break-up, and more. For me it was cancer. When you're in the middle of a crisis, it is difficult to imagine that you will get past it, recover and end up in a better place. That is exactly why I have chosen to write my book and speak with others about how surviving an (almost) overwhelming challenge can have extraordinarily positive outcomes.

I wouldn't want anyone to go through what I did with cancer; however, I would like you to know what I learned along the way. It is *never* too late to change your life and also change the lives of other people.

—**Don Armstrong**, author of *Finish YOUR Race: Empower Your Life with Strategies from a Cancer Survivor*

A Community of Support and Information

At the age of twenty-seven, I was on my way to becoming a successful opera singer. One morning I woke up and passed out due to a fever of 104°. Seven different infections raged through my body. It took two years and countless, frustrating visits to specialists before I was diagnosed with the chronic disease lupus. Due to my symptoms, my dreams of becoming an opera singer were stolen from me. However, I refused to let lupus steal anything else from me. I still had no idea what lupus was; all I knew was there was no cure and that my life had changed forever. I had so many questions about the disease, but could not find any answers. I vowed that no one should have to endure what I did. With my mom, Debbie, I founded the nonprofit Molly's Fund Fighting Lupus (MFFL) in 2007 to raise awareness of lupus, give patients a voice, and provide a community of support and information. Today, hundreds of thousands of lupus patients turn to MFFL for answers, for support, and for a friend.

—**Molly McCabe**

Overcoming Chronic Pain

When I was twenty-five years old, something happened that stopped me in my tracks. I was healthy, active, and creating a happy and meaningful life for myself. I had finally left a very difficult family situation. At the time, I was living with my boyfriend and had recently left my job as a foster care caseworker to pursue a master's degree in social work.

Because I wanted to join my boyfriend and a friend of his on a bicycling trip in Europe, I needed to get in shape so I began running. Soon, my back started bothering me. I went to a doctor who advised me to stop running and gave me some back exercises. However, everything I tried to do seemed to make the pain worse. I joined a yoga class but the teacher gave poor instructions and I hurt my back even more. After that, I was in agonizing pain 24/7. I could barely even sit in a chair to eat, and eventually dropped out of graduate school.

For the next three and a half years, I barely functioned because of the pain. Sometime in the middle of all this my boyfriend kicked me out and I was left with no way to support myself. I consulted with many doctors who couldn't find anything wrong with me. They put me on many different drugs including anti-inflammatories, muscle relaxants, and narcotics. I was like a zombie, and the drugs didn't help my pain. I saw a chiropractor who helped a little, then an osteopath who told me to stay in bed until I felt better and do nothing except see him for spinal manipulation. I spent six weeks in bed and felt even worse. My emotional state wasn't helped because I was spending so much time in bed.

I had spiraled deep into despair and was having suicidal thoughts when a friend recommended that I read a book about the mind/body connection. The book was by a man who healed himself from a progressive, very painful degenerative joint disease with laughter. Until that point, I had no idea that what was in my mind affected my body. The book mentioned biofeedback, which uses sensitive instruments to measure physiology and provides the information to help the patients learn to control their bodies. I decided to find a biofeedback therapist.

At my first biofeedback session, the therapist explained how fear and worry created more pain and instructed me in relaxation techniques to manage my thoughts while he measured the results with biofeedback. He sent me home with a biofeedback device that wrapped around my finger and measured my hand temperature, a measure of stress. My pain decreased 50 percent in a day! I was shocked, and also a little hopeful. I thought I would never have control over the pain that was attacking my body. But the psychologist taught me that I was helping to create the pain and I could learn to control it.

I started measuring my hand temperature throughout the day and doing relaxation techniques to stay in the relaxed range, and within a short time I was feeling well enough to get back to work. I wasn't entirely pain free yet and that was my goal.

I went to a health spa where a psychologist was teaching the guests how to use self- hypnosis to lose weight. I asked her if she could show me how to use hypnosis for pain relief. After talking with me she said that my pain was from all of the emotions I had never processed about things that had happened to me in my past, including anger at my mother and grief over past relationships. She taught me how to use self-hypnosis to get in touch with and express my feelings about these events. I used what she taught me every day for more than a year and I started feeling pretty good. Not only was I letting go of my anger, grief, and pain, I was becoming a more compassionate person.

Things were going pretty well for me for a few years until I developed a bone spur on my foot in my big toe joint that caused a sharp pain with every step. After more conserva-tive measures to deal with it failed, I had surgery to remove the bone spur. Unfortunately, after the surgery I developed a different kind of foot pain that got worse and worse over time, to the point that I could not walk more than a block without severe pain. I was even having trouble putting my foot on the floor when I was sitting in a chair.

The mind/body treatments that had helped me with my back were useless with my foot pain. I went from doctor to doctor looking for a solution but no one could figure out what was wrong with me. I hobbled around for fourteen years unable to walk or stand for any length of time. Finally, someone suggested that I try Rolfing, very deep bodywork that stretches out muscles, tendons and the underlying tissues known as fascia to restore normal balance to the body. After just two sessions of Rolfing, I felt like I had a new foot. It turns out that when I was healing from my surgery I was walking on the side of my foot to prevent aggravating the incision and that caused a shortening of the soft tissue on one side of my foot and leg.

From these experiences, I've learned that there are different kinds of pain that require different solutions. It is unfortunate that most of the medical establishment doesn't understand pain and doesn't offer appropriate solutions to patients. It's been thirty-nine years since my first episode of chronic pain and I've had other pain and health challenges along the way. I've realized that doctors trained to use pharmaceuticals and surgical procedures have little understanding of the causes of chronic pain and often harm more than they help. Patients stumble around looking for help and only occasionally find the right treatment.

I knew that I could help people with chronic pain and illness. I left my job in 1993, got certified, and developed a practice for patients suffering, much as I had for so many years. My mission is to help people with pain quickly find safe and effective treatments—and never to give up, no matter what! It is wonderful when I hear from patients I've worked with or people who have read my book that I have helped them.

—**Cindy Perlin**, author *of The Truth About Chronic Pain*
Treatments: The Best and Worst Strategies
for Becoming Pain Free

Stones in a Jar

When my mother was dying of cancer, at first I could not accept that I would lose my other parent to the same disease that took my father. Also, I was finally pregnant with the grandchild my mother had always wanted. I put colored stones in one jar, each representing a day until my due date. We would take one out each day and put it in another jar so we could see how many were left. She died with 180 stones still left. At first, I was mad at the 180 stones. Just eighteen more days and she could have seen her grandchild. But then I realized it was 180 days when she didn't have to be in pain.

Then, I was able to accept it and look at the open door. Helen Keller said, "When one door of happiness closes, another opens, but often we look so long at the closed door that we do not see the one which has been opened for us." I accepted the door with life with my mother had closed and I needed to look at the open door (life with my son). I wrote my memoir of the experiences, which was great therapy, and I now speak in public to help people find their OPEN DOOR. Open hearts, open minds, and open doors.

—**Kelly Frankenberg**

The Power of Words

I had several low points but probably the lowest was when I was squatting in a foreclosed home, fat, depressed, alone, and suicidal. I had lost millions of dollars in a Ponzi scheme and then moved out of state to get work and ended up in a friend's house. He moved out, the house went into foreclosure, and I stayed there.

It was February 2009 and I didn't know if I could press forward. I felt abandoned and in the depths of despair I was considering suicide. I looked in the mirror and I decided that I could love life and would never give up. I consciously made a decision and spoke those powerful words aloud.

I wrote a contract to myself, saying that I would lose fifty pounds over the next 100 days. I got rid of all the junk food in the house and went out to get affordable, healthy food the next day. I started my fitness regimen; I had to be at work at 4 a.m. so I got up to do my cardio at 2 a.m. Then, I got a second job and began thinking about starting my own business.

I was on my own for about three and a half months and then moved to Idaho where I lived in my brother's treehouse. I had lost forty-seven pounds of body fat and my confidence and self-image had improved. Once I got to Idaho, I started thinking more positively, which led to positive actions. After about a year in the treehouse, I moved out and got my own apartment.

I set another ambitious goal. With the help of a fitness coach, I had seven weeks to become as buff as a bodybuilder. Again, by sticking to a regimen, I went from 13 percent body fat to 4.5 percent body fat. I motivated myself by putting photos of bodybuilders around the apartment. When I reached my goal, the photographer said I looked better than the body-builder on the magazine cover.

Meanwhile, people began telling me they had heard about my story and my physical transformation so I started sharing my journey.

My message is fairly simple. Overcoming challenges takes place when your thoughts become your words. Your words become actions. Actions become a habit. And a habit becomes your lifestyle or how you live.

The story of my physical transformation was featured online and led to attention from all around the world. My story was inspiring people all over; I didn't realize I had a story. I was just trying to live.

I had made changes and I was doing things that got me massive success. I used that as a launching pad for Samson Wear. Even when I couldn't keep selling "Never give up" on my tee-shirts for the company, I knew that I could keep going. I began building the Samson Wear company; the body-building gave me the strength and courage to overcome my challenges. And hope and positive words kept me going. That ultimately is the message that I want to spread to everyone.

I've become an expert on the power of words. I look at everything in a positive light. And when I'm asked whether there is a formula to making changes, I say you need to be doing things on a daily basis, not weekly or monthly. Consistency, persistence, and dedication are the keys to accomplishing what you want. We have developed the Samson LIFE Challenge that is a three-pillar program based on small tasks related to wisdom (connections and happiness), wellness (nutrition and fitness), and wealth (abundance and dreams)

We've studied the richest and most successful leaders for the past three decades and incorporated their strategies into our program. We have had amazing success: saving people from suicide, inspiring depressed teens to become empowered, couples growing closer, and lots more.

Now I speak and I'm working on a second book in addition to my program that develops leadership habits in teens and individuals. I want to help people do better in life and transform themselves.

I have the cool mission to share the power of words with other people. Words can bring life and death. I want them to bring life and abundance, not despair and destruction.

Everything begins with a decision. There is no difference between small decisions and big ones. You go through the process and then map out a plan. I made a decision to live and then I made a decision to make my company successful.

Without my contract, I would have slipped back. Everyone can make a decision that you can commit to. We train people on how to accumulate wealth. You can give them the simplest and the best plan. They want the home or car or freedom but if they don't make a decision and commitment to do what's necessary to reach those goals, they won't get there. Words help you create action, and that is powerful.

—Rocky Detwiler, founder of Samson LIFE;
author of *The Samson Effect: Transforming Lives
with the Power of Words*

There Is Still Love in His Smiles

My heart has been filled with love since the day I met Ken. Our lives were complicated and after ten years together we were married. Our happily-ever-after dream crashed, along with his van, after a diagnosis of Frontotemporal dementia. I care for him and love him more every day. I watch him vanish before my eyes, slowly, very slowly, but still feel the love in his smiles. He is mostly nonverbal and can barely walk, but I wouldn't trade this love for anything else in the world. Dementia creates a new way for love to be shared.

—Rona Klein

Becoming Purpose Driven

After the loss of four siblings, one mentally challenged, I suffered from severe depression. Add divorce after twenty years, children graduated and on their own. I didn't know how to process all the grief and loss. I had to decide what to do with the rest of my life. My son gave me an Open Heart necklace.

Every time I looked at it and remembered what it meant, my heart opened. I was inspired to be an example to my kids and others. Fate led me to a position in mental health. Last year, I graduated from the Neighborhood Leadership Institute where I learned ways to impact my community. Now I volunteer as a benefits counselor helping people apply for assistance; I also feed the homeless and tutor students. I'm also getting a degree in social work so I can serve various populations. My passion is advocating for changes in policies to make them welcoming and simpler to seek assistance. My life has gone from depression to purpose driven all because I opened my heart and light came in.

—Anonymous

Creating Opportunities

I am a survivor of molestation, physical abuse, illiteracy, and poverty. I am the first in my family to graduate from high school, and I went on to graduate school. It is my passion to create programs that will create opportunities for people who grew up like me. Because of my passion, I created Urban Fitness 911 to address the disparity of health, fitness, and academics in low-income communities. It is a total wellness program that emphasizes lifelong exercise, healthy cooking and nutrition, academic tutoring, and inspirational experiences with amazing people and places in the community. We have already seen how this comprehensive model can work.

By giving these students respect, focused attention, and new experiences, they start to see who they can be. We are helping 100 students every week, with 15 to 20 hours of programming.

—Dr. Veronica Everett-Boyce

Part Two

Families Come in Different Shapes and Sizes

Family is not just the one in which you were born but the one you create by opening your heart to those who you can love and help. These stories show how important family is and how you can create your own "community" of loved ones to expand your family or to build your own out of necessity. From children helping elderly neighbors to colleagues at work or strangers who bond together to help one another, everyone can be part of a loving community. We grew up that way— our family always opened our hearts and our home to those in need. Subsequently they would become family and a source of comfort in our time of need.

Transforming a Child's Life
and Helping the Family and Community

Eleven years ago, I produced a Public Service Announcement
for a wheelchair organization. Afterward, Chris Lewis (Jerry's
son), who knew that my wife and I were adopting a child from
Ethiopia, told me about a scheduled trip to deliver wheelchairs
in that country. I went there and saw for myself the reality of
Third World countries. People had crawled or carried toddlers
for days to the distribution center. Some people didn't even
know if they could get to keep the wheelchairs.

When I returned home, someone contacted me about a
paraplegic in Ethiopia named Ephrem who needed a specialty
wheelchair. This request led to me to David Richard, who was
customizing wheelchairs for the most severely injured—"the
forgotten of the forgotten." We connected via email and within
days, he had Ephrem's "new ride" ready, for free. This type of
wheelchair would have cost $3,000 to $5,000, which would
obviously be prohibitive for someone who earns approximately $300 a year. Ephrem (whom David and I later had the
joy and honor of meeting in person) was able to get around
instead of being bedridden. He kept calling his new wheelchair "his Mercedez"!

David (one of the world's foremost advocates on global
disability) didn't ask me for a donation even though I knew he
and his organization could use the money. He actually didn't
ask me for *anything*. I soon learned he had already helped give
away some 200,000 wheelchairs around the world in sixty-
plus countries, mostly to children and elderly folks. Once

David and I met, we became immediate friends, and to this day I consider him my mentor in caring and giving and in the true purpose of life.

Having a 24/7 LA-based ad agency when I met David kept me quite busy and often stretched. But it also thankfully allowed me the ability to create videos, photos, and marketing materials for David and his wheelchair mission. In addition, David's "seating clinics" to more than sixty countries left him physically exhausted, and he was also suffering from a severe and debilitating illness. We went for a ride on our motorcycles, our favorite pastime together, and sat on a bluff overlooking the Pacific Ocean and started talking about starting our own nonprofit. We listed all the logical reasons why this wasn't smart, why we could fail, why, why, why.... It's amazing how the objections can fill your head like a tidal wave when there is always a better answer...if you are just willing to look for it....Aside from asking my wife to marry me some fifteen years earlier, I asked David the most important question of my life. "Will more children be in a better place if we do this or not?" "Instantly all of our rational objections fell away. David looked at me with more energy and passion I had seen from him in years and said, "Drew, we need to do this. We must do this. We *will* do this." And at that moment, on a bluff overlooking endless waters and a spectacular sunset about to chart our course, we decided to go for it. In 2012, we created Global Mobility. David was completely re-energized and immediately full of ideas on how to get cooperation from donors, corporations, and medical teams. He even had this "farfetched" idea about how we could get worldwide shipping giant DHL to help ship our wheelchairs around the world...for *free*. (And yes, that happened, and DHL now does that for us. THANK YOU, DHL, FOR YOUR OPEN HEARTS!!!)

People often ask me how or why I am involved with Global Mobility. I tell them, you only need to see one child on the ground and look in their eyes and see how the child comes back to life the moment they are seated in their first wheelchair. Or you'll look at a parent who sees his or her precious child in that wheelchair, *off* the ground for the first time in their life, and trust me, you'll be hooked. We want to help one child at a time. When we deliver the wheelchairs, we spend three to four hours with each child and have doctors and occupational therapists with us. We provide a tutorial and tools so the family can maintain and repair the wheelchair.

I've learned from all of my journeys with Global Mobility and from my dear friend and mentor David Richard that when you're responding from the heart, not from a place of ego, you can move quickly, efficiently, and genuinely. There's no huge decision-making process at Global Mobility. The vast majority of the money donated or raised is used for the wheelchairs. We didn't want to create a large organization with bureaucracy and politics; we have very low overhead and we don't have major marketing expenses. The doctors who travel with us around the world pay their own way; in fact, they often shut their own medical practices to make the trips. (Thank you, Doctor Eric Munro!) When I'm traveling for Global Mobility, I cover my expenses. As it should be.

We've seen what a difference we can make in improving lives and now we're partnering with other groups. For example, in Guatemala, we have partnered with Pacific Dental to offer free dental clinics and we work with ETHIOPIA SMILES and HUMBLE.ORG to provide free dental care and toothbrushes to children and their families. We work globally with individual NGOs, churches, religious organizations, hospitals, local governments, and so forth.

I run a large worldwide ad agency so my schedule is packed. I have four children, three of whom are infants. I am fortunate and want to help other children around the world. Meeting David has changed my life dramatically. Not a day goes by when I don't think back to many of the kids that we've helped. When we give a child a wheelchair, we're helping the child, his family, and the community. A wheelchair is truly life-changing for the whole family and the community. I can't adequately describe what it's like to see men, women, and children crawling on the ground....and the difference in their eyes, hearts, and souls when they receive their wheelchairs. One boy named Bryan in Guatemala who received a wheelchair from us was able to return to school; now he plans to become a doctor and give back.

There are no bad days when you do what we do.

—**Drew Plotkin**, GobalMobilityUSA.org,
2017 Open Hearts Honoree

Staying in Touch

Family is just one word. But that word encompasses an abundance of meanings. For me, family began as the people with whom I lived and extended out to my grandparents, aunts, uncles, and cousins. By the time I was eight years old, though, I only had one grandfather, one uncle, and two cousins. My mother is an only child, and my father had one half-brother. Since that uncle and his two sons lived many states away, my immediate family turned to each other, and our genetic bonds grew even stronger through our shared experiences.

I remember the big events our family experienced, but I also remember the little things too. Things like water gun fights in the back yard when the summer heat had become almost unbearable. Or the flour battles in the kitchen with Mom while we were baking pies and teasing each other. How about playing Monopoly by candlelight when the power went out for several hours one evening, and we had nothing else to do. And I can't forget the general awareness of my family when I was having a bad day. We knew when one of us needed something a little extra to get us through the day. And I owe them a lot for contributing to the woman I am now.

No, we weren't always together, and there were countless times when we argued or even avoided each other. But what relationship doesn't come with its ups and downs? It's what you do during the down times that makes or breaks the longevity of that relationship. If you shut down and close yourself off, you ruin the chance to repair any damage that's been done. My parents instilled in us from childhood that friends come and go, but family will always be there, whether we like it or not. It's our choice what we do with that fact.

There are many people out there with brothers and sisters, even parents, from whom they haven't heard in years. When I meet someone who tells me that, it astounds me. I can't even begin to imagine not talking to my parents or my brothers for more than a week, let alone years. It's true: life gets busy, other things place high demands on our time, and as we get older, we can naturally drift apart. And yes, family will hurt you, sometimes quite deeply. In those instances, it's easy to turn your back and close the door to the pain. If you do, you run the risk of severing the relationship forever. But, that won't happen if you make a conscious effort to prevent it from occurring.

To me, family is just like love. It's an active, daily choice to maintain the relationship and help it grow stronger. You can choose to allow life to get in the way, or you can choose to pick up the phone and call them, or get in the car and drive to see them if they live close enough. In this day of email, Skype, text messages, and cellphones, it takes but a minute to make that connection.

I now live 2,000 miles from my family. I have a husband, two children, and a whole new life that's separate from them. Yet, I still email, text, or call them at least once a week. Through good times and bad, my family means far too much to me to let them go.

—Tiffany Amber Stockton

Caregiving

My parents moved to Maui in 1989, after my dad retired. They wanted to "watch their grandkids grow up." But when they moved so far away from other family and friends, they were stuck. At age ninety or so, they couldn't take any more trips to visit mainland friends and family. As a result, my brother Andy had the responsibility of doing what my parents wanted most—keeping them in their home and out of an assisted living facility.

I visited when I could, but the day-to-day was squarely on my brother's shoulders. For years, he handled the cooking, shopping, doctor appointments, and even thwarting con men telemarketers from fleecing them out of their money.

Getting calls in the night: "Dad fell. Come quick." "I think Mother had a stroke. Can you come?" It was draining, frustrating, heartbreaking, and at times, unbearable. The parents become the children, and how do you walk that fine line of maintaining your increasingly demented father's dignity when he feels his mortality 24/7, all his friends are gone, and in the dead of night he tries to talk your mother into committing suicide with him?

Finally, the call from my brother came. "Dad is going into hospice." I jumped on a plane immediately. I pulled up to the facility, and there was this handsome white-haired man. "Oh my God!" I thought, "It's Andy. His hair had gone pure white!" Andy. The funny one. The one my Dad always referred to as "George Bailey" from *It's a Wonderful Life*. And how true. Just like George, Andy gave up many of his own hopes and dreams to be there for others.

He was pacing and crying. He grabbed me tight. "Thank God you're here. Thank God. Please, Sue, I am not even joking when I tell you that I feel like this is killing me. Dad's babbling, saying the TV is reading his mind...I feel like I'm going to have a stroke and die right here in the parking lot. I'm scared. I have a family too!" And there it was. My brother hit the wall, right in front of my eyes. I told him, "I will take it from here. I won't let them call you for anything while I'm on this island. You go sleep, get drunk, scream into a pillow, whatever it takes. You are off duty." I thought I'd lose two people that day.

Sixteen days later Dad was gone. Andy saw it through to the end, like the good man he is. What a toll it takes on the ones who love us to death. When Dad passed, I thought to myself, "He's free. We are all free."

—**Sue Clark**

I Am Who I Am Because of My Family

Through my teen years into adulthood I have always tried to take different traits from each of my family members and mold them into the person that I wanted to become. My dad is a retired Philadelphia fireman, and the trait that I have taken from him is "bravery." As a child, I never realized the risks and dangers of his job. At any moment without hesitation he would answer the call of duty to save something or someone, all the while putting his life in harm's way. From my mom I took the trait of "being level-headed." She has always been the one in our family that I could go to when things were going wrong or not the way I wanted them to go. In a calm and logical way, she would help me to weigh the situation and remind me to take every challenge and turn it into a blessing. The trait that I took from my brother Charlie is to "live life to its fullest." To find the joy in everything, whether it is finding a career you are passionate about or scuba diving in Honduras with sharks. Don't let anything hold you back from enjoying and living a full life. Finally, what I took from my sister Cathi was "compassion." My sister has dedicated her life to taking care of the sick as an RN. I am always amazed at how loving and compassionate she is and how she truly cares for each patient with whom she works. The time that she takes getting to know these people, listening to them, and letting them know that they are not alone is remarkable. I only hope that I have taken these traits from my family and have put them to good use and made my family proud. Because in the end, it all boils down to I am the person I have become because of my family. Without them, I am nothing. And I hope that someday my children will take some of these traits and become brave, level-headed, happy, and compassionate human beings and turn this world into an even more loving place. And it will be all thanks to their family for showing them the way.

—**Tara L. Moyer**

My Adopted Grandma

I was born, raised, and educated in a Canadian city in Manitoba. I only remember visiting with my true grandparents two summers: once when I was nine and once when I was thirteen. I fell in love with them dearly; but because they lived in Portugal, thousands of miles away, it wasn't possible to visit with them at regular intervals. And because they lived in a small town with no phone, I couldn't speak to them regularly.

However, God had something special in store for my sister and me—a neighbor. We met Mrs. Barbara McDonald when I was around eight years old and my sister was eleven. The interesting thing was that Mrs. McDonald had only two granddaughters, who were our ages exactly, and they lived thousands of miles from her. She soon became our "adopted grandmother." She took us shopping and bought us small toys and cut-out dolls. True to her name, she was the first person ever to take my sister and me to McDonalds. But the most important thing about her was that she taught us about the love of God and "family." When I needed someone to talk to, someone just to be with, or someone to pray for me, she was always available.

Luckily, she was with me for many years; and, she was a part of my "family" when I was growing up, and even after I married. She passed away on the day my sister had her third child. I had visited her that day; she was in a coma. I told her that my sister had just had a little girl named Sabrina. You know what? I really do believe she heard me. I thanked her for always being there for me, and I said goodbye.

"Grandma," I miss you still today! Thanks for being with me always.

Love, Izzy

—Isabel Sebastiao-Vieira

Family of the Heart

Families come in all shapes and sizes. There is the nuclear family of parents and children. There is the birth family. And there is the family of the heart.

For twenty-nine years, my husband and I have belonged to a dinner club. Our dinner club consists of six couples who gather every month at the home of members. We are a casual group, with the host and hostess providing the main dish and assigning appetizers, salads, and desserts.We have seen each other through the births of babies and the deaths of parents. We have weathered illnesses, including cancer, hip replacements, and others. We celebrate each other's successes and weep over the hurts that beset all of us. We support each other in an infinite variety of ways, including fasting and praying when one of our dear friends was diagnosed with leukemia last year.

Last year, we said a temporary goodbye to one of our couples who left to serve a mission for our church. They are still part of our group, in our thoughts, in our prayers, in our hearts.

Our dinner club group is family in the best sense, bound by memories, by grief, and, most of all, by love.

—Anonymous

The FIRM Believers Club

In the year that I have been a part of the FIRM Believers Club, I have had a chance to chat with the wonderful instructors and along the way have forge some great friendships with fellow believers. All of us there are women young and old who have been through lots in our lives: cancer, birth, ailing spouses, loss of life, and so on. We are all there for each other through the thick and thin, supporting each other, and giving each other encouragement daily. Each one of those women that I've become friends with feels like much more than a friend to me, even though most of us are all spread out. They are my cheering section, the reassurance when I have a set back and the inspiration than even with life deals you a bad hand you can rise above and have some wonderful people right there with you.

—Sarah Buchanan

We Hug and We Cry

For me, living with an Open Heart definitely makes it easier to accept bad things. I changed my thinking from: "Why me and Why did this happen to me?" into "Why not me?" I can't change what happened. I have to accept it and find a way to get through it.

Facing Papa's death in February is definitely the worst I could imagine having to experience. All of a sudden, my family's life changed completely. The entire family is still trying to find a way to get through this. With only Mama, Gina, and me left in the house, it's sometimes hard for me to stand the silence. My radio is playing nearly all the time. Reading the *Open Heart* books again makes me feel better. And I find comfort in helping others.

We're trying to help a friend of ours who had been sober for about five years but is now having problems with alcohol again. I try to comfort his pregnant wife while he stays in the clinic. We talk, we are silent, we hug, and we cry. Last week she told me that she couldn't believe that I'm doing all this with her while I'm still grieving so badly over Papa. I told her about Open Hearts and gave her my copy of *The Wave* and put a note on page 12 that said, "We are family." She called me two days later, telling me that she is so thankful I gave it to her.

Both of our families will be able to find a way to get through our challenges. It will take some time, but I'm sure it will happen.

—**Wiebke Prasuhn**

Sharing My Life and Open Heart

My adversity was my singleness. In my twenties, I had my plans: marriage, children, and a nursing career. But I never married and so desperately wanted to have children. It never happened. In my fifties, looking back, my life has contained none of those things. I never married, never had my own children, and career-wise, I have been in office management. Currently, I am one of three managers in a retirement community.

I spent thirty years working with teenagers (these were my children) running church youth programs, directing youth camps, leading mission trips for teens to Third World countries, and more! I have been so blessed by the hundreds of teens with whom I have been allowed to share my life and open heart.

Now I am pouring myself into helping retirees. I love getting to know them and their stories and making their "home" a pleasant place.

Would I still have liked to be married and have my own family? Sure! But as I have learned to be content and accept the twists my life has taken, I forgive myself for perceived failures and use my life to pour into others, which makes me feel so good. I am thankful for the fullness of my life.

—**Debra Rodgers**

Providing a Helping Hand

My partner and I have been together for fifteen years now. We have always wanted to have a large family of our own. Throughout the years we have had the opportunity to help lots of people who needed a helping hand. We are always the type to give someone a helping hand when needed. In 2009, we were introduced to a young lady who wanted to place her unborn child up for adoption and we immediately offered our home to her unborn child. Since then we have had the opportunity to have her extended family become part of our extended family. Just recently, a neighbor hit hard times and needed someplace for her four children to stay in a safe environment. After six fun-filled weeks these children are thriving under our roof. Although this is only temporary, we are excited to share our love with these children. We are also very excited about the opportunity to become foster parents in order to offer our home and love to as many children and families as we can touch.

—**Anonymous**

Caring for Others

In 2007, I lost my seventeen-year-old son. I tried to return to my life, but I just couldn't seem to pull my life together. My mother owned a disabled veterans home and was in poor health. She was dying so I moved in with her to keep her business going and keep her out of a nursing home. I cared for six disabled veterans and my mother. My heart, even though broken, became open through loving and caring for these vets and my mother. Mother has passed but the home remains open because I opened my heart.

—**Bonnie Hayslip**

Helping Others Communicate

The empowering deed that brings me the most joy is assisting hearing-impaired people. I'm a CART provider for the hearing impaired. CART stands for computer assisted real-time translation. I provide real-time translation in public settings, from school lectures to church services to meetings. Providing communication for these individuals so they are able participate with others is such a great feeling for me. I was told by people I work with that the service I'm providing gives them the opportunity to be part of the community. Without it, they feel lost and isolated.

By experiencing other people's predicaments and how they handle situations has given me a different outlook in life. This knowledge embraces me to have openness in my mind, heart, and spirit. In my opinion, the act of sharing, learning, and giving can be felt by everyone around you. As I do these acts, I know it helps people in their day-to-day lives. With this awareness, I live with an "open heart" every day.

—Anonymous

Donating an Organ

Four years ago, my dear friend Patricia was in stage four kidney failure. She began dialysis three times per week. After three-and-a-half years her body was wearing out. I first opened my mind and heart to the possibility of donating my kidney. Last year about this time we began our journey. After several months of medical testing we were cleared for surgery. On June 16, 2016, I donated my kidney and my dear friend is now enjoying life again. On the day of the surgery she presented me with my Open Heart necklace! A perfect gift! Love it!

—Diane Beard

The Grace of a Swan

Recently, I have had the honor of organizing a special "Angel Mission Fund" for a very dear high school girlfriend of mine. Kathy was diagnosed almost three years ago with ALS (Lou Gehrig's disease). She has endured more physical and medical obstacles then most of us will ever encounter in our lifetime.

I raised enough funds to take Kathy to NYC for her very special "Make a Wish Weekend." We did everything that her little heart desired, and what she could do physically—Broadway plays, Hudson River dinner cruises, museums, and more. We stayed in a wonderful hotel in the heart of Times Square. It was an all-girl weekend and so much fun.

Although she was extremely exhausted by the end of the weekend, Kathy was a trooper and was not going to let her disease stand in her way of enjoying what she loves most—Life!! She had a wonderful weekend, and it filled my heart with so much joy to see her smile through all her pain.

Kathy has amazing strength. Although she faces daily challenges, she rises with the sun every morning and has the grace of a beautiful swan, ready for a new day. She is my hero and her courage is endless.

—**Mindy Loftus**

Change One Little Thing for the Better

I retired from a career in public schools. To celebrate, my husband and I went to Jamaica, supposedly for fun in the sun. He spent the week repairing medical equipment in the very sad local hospital. I spent a portion of the week at an elementary school. It changed us in a good way! In fact, we are going back in a few weeks, me laden with school supplies and him toting tools and test equipment. If we can change one little thing for the better, we are in the right place! Peace.

—**Jane Sandona**

Never Give Up on Anything

Ruth Kepner is a strong woman. She is blind and has other health issues but that does not stop her from doing anything. She has a huge heart towards everyone. She taught me never to give up on anything in life as it is a precious gift from God. She is like a mom to me. I lived with her for two years and we took care of each other. We would go out to lunch and shopping and even to each other's doctor's appointments. Her son drove us since neither of us can drive. She lives in Maine and I moved to Colorado ten years ago. But I still call her to make sure she is doing well, and I visit her whenever I am in Maine visiting my children. I am disabled and she showed me you can do anything if you try hard enough. Because of that, I teach my grandchildren and children to never think negatively about what you want out of life. Keep your heart open to yourself and others and you can be certain that the road through life will always be the right one.

—**Anonymous**

Love, Forgive, and Move On

I am seventeen years old and my life didn't start out well. I was in foster care for years and then adopted. My brother died by suicide in April of this year. I have never had grandparents, uncles, or aunts. But through all this I have found a way to love, forgive, and move on. I have found out that, if I keep my heart open to love and not hate towards people, I am much happier. I have volunteered with underprivileged kids who live in the horrible part of town and don't have really good homes or people who care about them. Helping them get a second chance at life brings love to my heart. I have been there with friends through the bad times and often lost them when I needed them. And that's okay. Through all this my present was Jesus, family, love, and peace.

—Carolyn Wren

Generosity and Compassion

I have a wonderful example from the life of my ninety-two-year-old mother, Viola, of an open heart, open mind philosophy. She grew up with little, but has lived her life with generosity and compassion. She befriended people with mental disabilities and gave them rides to church and took them out to lunch. Hitchhikers passing our home would be treated to dinner, showers, a new set of clothes, and a little cash. I have benefited having her for a role model of what empathy and "love thy neighbor" truly means. I am blessed by inheriting her open heart. Thanks, Mom.

—Sandra Kleman

Journeying Through an Open Heart in Search of My Words

The emotions abounded through my heart as my eyes witnessed the outline of a faint cloud of love pulling with such strength from my body as I breathed in their beauty wrapped in the tiny, pink, fluffy outfits they laid within, their delicate limbs kicking, grasping at their new world. I turned to my mom, held her closely, deeply, and with gratitude I spoke, "Mom, I love you more today than I could have ever imagined. Through all that I have been ungrateful for, you loved me to a degree in which I never knew existed until this moment." And as my mom would always respond, "I know dear. I know." And she kissed me gently on my forehead. I responded, "I love you more than all the stars in the universe." This was the morning of the birth of my twins.

As an only child, my mother and I have always been close. However, as I was raising my twins, my mother was diagnosed with schizophrenia. Overnight, I suddenly faced a multitude of family, social, and financial problems. The trials and tribulations poured over me like a tropical storm upon a small boat. I could not find my way to shore. I was lost, a single mom raising small children while caring for a mentally and physically ill parent was an emotionally draining experience. Who was this new mom? And how would I relate to the individual she'd become?

My friends gathered around me, gave me strength, and thanked me in abundance for the love and support I'd bestowed upon them over the years. They knew I'd been able to be strong for them, because I'd been given the gift of love from my mom and dad. They lifted me up when my wings had truly forgotten how to fly. I needed them and they were there for my family, for me.

On the morning of October 23, 2000, I wrote, in dedication to my friends, *"I Believe that Friends are Quiet Angels who lift us to our Feet when our Wings have trouble remembering how to Fly!"* I remember my heart being so full of love and thankfulness that morning. I was in God's presence. However, within twenty-four hours of authoring the dedication, it was taken from me and simply took on its own life online and in print.

Immediately, my voice became silent. I put down my writer's pen, and I chose to take responsibility as a mother and as a daughter and maintain the stability of my family. Approximately twenty-two months later I was diagnosed with a severe depressive disorder in addition to stage three breast cancer. I underwent treatment for both diagnoses while I continued to work, raise my girls, and tend to my parents in the evenings.

My life has been filled with maintaining my health, supporting other breast cancer survivors, caring for my parents through their aging years, and loving and guiding my twins into adulthood. My Angels (friends) and I are continuing to lift one another through our life's journeys. I thank God for them daily.

At this point in life I'm fortunate for the ability to embrace the truth of my existence. As a shy child, I was deeply in love with my mother; as a teenager, I didn't understand her or myself. I was rebellious of her love and her worth. As a young woman, I set out to find my purpose. I made mistakes. But, when I became a mother of twins I understood the immediacy and scope of my mother's love. Through life's lessons I've gained perspective. I've learned to accept each moment one breath at a time. To be where I am in that moment, I embrace the beauty and the love in that breath. I learned this from caring for my mom all those years. Because of this, I can relax and see her face and hear her laugh when I sit calmly and breathe. Because of this I can project the love and beauty in my life.

Recently, I began writing again and was advised to set up a website to present my work. I became curious about the path of my quote and researched it online. The images and references flashed in my face like a raging fire. My heart turned to stone. I felt its weight pushing through my chest cavity. Why had the world decided I was anonymous and felt it had the right to exploit my work? Then I burst into tears. I felt the burden of failure. The quote had ventured throughout the world with no one acknowledging me as the author. My colleague heard my muffled tears and pressed me and asked what I was going to do about it. I told her my story of how I had consulted an attorney in 2000, but had been naïve about protecting my words. I'd written the verse out of love and gratitude. It never occurred to me to sell it. However, its admirers were embracing it and understood its intent. Friends are the extension of yourself. They are a reflection of who you are as an individual and shine the most when you are in need. The brilliance of their love for you warms your soul when you are joyous.

Although I was angry with the world, I was furious with myself for not protecting my words legally. But the more I continued searching for the quote the more appreciative I became. I saw the creativity of its use. I saw beyond profit. I saw the need and love individuals were bestowing upon one another. And I asked myself, "Wasn't it my intent to share my love and gratitude? Aren't these individuals doing the same?" My heart melted. I became appreciative as opposed to resentful. I've seen my poem in inspirational stories, sermons, poetry, lesson plans, obituaries, headstones, holistic websites, sororities, and writings from nonprofit foundations. So many people have been impacted by my words. One minister stated he believed the author understood the value of friendship, and the value and trust of God's love. I am humbled by the accuracy of his analysis of my intent.

One of the attributes of the quote that I've recognized is the need of individuals to express their love for another human being and their need for friendship. Apparently, as I have realized, we cannot exist without the help of others. Friendship gives me peace and comfort. It is compassion and it nurtures my soul. When acts of kindness are bestowed upon me, I cry. I cry tears of gratefulness because someone cares about how I feel and about my needs, goals, and frustrations as a human-being. Someone cares.

Friendship is an open pathway to our hearts and souls. And I will continue to spread that message through the reemergence of my voice in my words and my ongoing writing.

—Lorraine Kay Mitchell

Part Three

Moving Past
a Family Crisis

To an observer, a family may appear perfect when in fact the family is in the midst of a very difficult time, whether it is an emotional crisis, or difficulty with a child, or some other catastrophe. We all face calamities but often they are manageable. In these stories, individuals who truly have suffered the unimaginable somehow found a way to get past these hard times and find a road ahead that will lead to better times. By sharing their experience and showing how they moved ahead, they are inspiring others to change things for the better.

Be Open and Share Your Story

Fourteen years ago, while I was pregnant with my son, my then husband was hospitalized for bipolar disorder. He was in and out of the hospital several times and ended up killing himself when my son was seven years old. We had been separated, but he died about a week before our divorce was to be finalized.

My former mother-in-law blamed me for her son's death, and that created many problems. She was very angry with me and wanted nothing to do with me; however, she still wanted a relationship with her grandson. The only problem with that was it had to be on her terms. I asked her to go to therapy so we could have a better relationship for my son. She refused! I knew that she had said critical things about me to my son, such as that I had been mean and that's why my husband killed himself. This led her to file a lawsuit trying to secure grandparent rights. We went to court, which took so much money, and in the end she still refused to go to therapy, which the court suggested as well. It was a very hard decision to limit my son's visits with her, but since my decision she has lost another grandson to an overdose.

My son was diagnosed with ADHD when he was in elementary school. It has been incredibly hard to try and undo the mess that was caused by living in the unstable bipolar world. You can't help but get caught up in it. One of my first steps to regain order in our lives came with the help of my mom and my cousin who lived with us for a short time. This allowed me to continue to work and try to bring back balance to our lives. It wasn't until my husband's death that I was able to start opening up about my past and sharing my experiences. Even at work (I'm a flight attendant), I would talk about my home life with a bipolar family member and sometimes people would ask me questions, saying they had similar situation in their family. I'm often asked how to recognize the signs of bipolar disease.

Being open and able to share has helped me move forward. I don't hide it. The problem we still have with mental illness is that we're not dealing with it. This disease deserves the same dedication for a cure as is given to cancer and many other illnesses. If we talk more about it and share our experiences, maybe we can erase the stigma.

I went to therapy for seven years while I was dealing with my late husband's disease. This therapy helped prepare me for when my son was diagnosed with ADHD. It also helped me deal with all the feelings you go through during life's highs and lows. My son is doing much better, but even today we both still experience struggles.

I'm now remarried and my husband has a wonderful daughter whom we love. My son has a great relationship with them both, and that stability has helped enormously. My husband has been instrumental in helping my son and I move forward. He is a great communicator and would listen and not judge me based on the past.

My biggest message for anyone going through a similar experience is to be open and share your story. Talking to different people is the best way to heal. You may or may not need therapy. If you don't talk to a therapist, then talk with a friend or a relative. Find that one person to talk to who will listen and give you honest answers.

—Laura Moore

Just Keep Putting One Foot in Front of the Other

My son Bo has had addiction problems since he was age thirteen. I believe addiction is a disease; he has the pre-disposition and had a need for getting high. He was in county jails five times and in state prison, but he has now been sober for five years.

I didn't realize there was alcoholism in my immediate family. Bo has addiction on each side of his parents' families. Some members are in AA. I joined Al-Anon twenty-seven years ago and I believe it saved my life.

When I divorced, the children were about ages nine and three and the court split them up. Back then, I thought if I can survive that, then I can go on. After all, some of my friends were going through much worse situations with their kids suffering from cancer or even dying. I couldn't sit there and complain. I was a daughter, mother, sister and best friend. No one wants to be around Wendy the whiner. I had to do what I had do. I didn't want my son's issues to ruin my second marriage or my daughter's childhood. Most of all, I didn't want my parents constantly worrying.

When he was loaded, Bo was awful and a real pain. I couldn't stand to be near him when he was using. I had to remind myself that he is sick and not dead, at least not yet. I had to find a *level of acceptance*. That's all you can do. I'm a normie, meaning I don't have any addictive behaviors.

You can't try to understand an addict because you won't be able to. Addicts are not rational: Why would anyone spend rent money on drugs if the rent is due? Drugs own you once you're addicted. My son's addictions got so bad that he stole from me. That was his personal low. I never thought he would rob me, but he did. He was in a lot of trouble because he had been on a four-day bender and he ended up getting picked up by the police at a shady motel. I was lucky he was alive.

When a family member is an addict, the fear and stress is incredibly difficult and can destroy the entire family unit. I don't like the word "hope" and it was scary to have it, but I believed he could make this work. Bo tried to commit suicide several times following stays in psychiatric hospitals. He was also in several car accidents and again he survived. He served extended periods of time in jail but he survived. You cannot punish an addict by incarceration. Rehabilitation is much more successful but only if the addict is willing. My son wasn't willing at all.

I was a wife with two children, and I had to believe that Bo would beat the odds and beat his addiction. I couldn't allow myself to think that he would continue to use drugs and alcohol and die.

His lowest point was in June 2007. He had been in jail and was then released but ended up back in. Who goes back to jail? I was horrified. One night I was so angry after he attempted to kill himself I told him that if he was really serious about dying, could he please overdose in front of UCLA so that his organs could be donated. I accepted long ago that addicts don't make smart choices but I was tired of watching him throw his life away. I said that he was killing me by wasting his time at rehab and drug programs. I said to him, "If you don't want to recover, I can't deal with this anymore."

I was never going to give up on him. I did, however, want to scare him enough to think I might. I brought him into the world. He didn't ask to become an addict. I certainly didn't sign up either! I reminded myself his illness could be worse; Bo was sick but not a bad person. Bo has severe OCD and ADHD so adding meth with ADHD medication made the problem even worse.

I stayed with Bo twice at a California state prison up north. We had a small apartment to share, and I stayed three nights and four days. He was really sick and incredibly fragile. Thin and sad, he was using drugs in prison. He still wanted to die and was too afraid to hang himself so he used a friend's meds and a dirty needle. As a result, he contracted hepatitis C. We had long chats while we sat on the prison couch. I was heartbroken but I was now more determined to find great doctors to help when he was released. I was committed to saving him from himself. I told him my plan. He was happy; he was tired of being dependent on drugs.

It was really, really hard going to court hearings and knowing he would be immediately sent to jail. I visited him every week and talked to him through a pane of glass. We held our hands and touched through the thick pane of glass. There were no hugs or kisses. When I said good-by, I blew a kiss promising him that I would be back the next week. If I didn't go to visit, he would think he wasn't worth visiting. He was and is my heart. I went until he was transferred to prison where he served seven years and eight months.

Finally, Bo's best friend got married and became a father. The friend met Bo at one of his rehab stays and told Bo that he couldn't be part of his family if he was still using drugs. That was *the* defining moment, and Bo said he had to stop using in prison and get his life together or face spending the rest of his life behind bars. Now, he is out and has a job he loves. He is good at it. I see how kind and thoughtful he can be when he is drug free.

I have suffered from clinical depression for eight years. It runs in my family as well as Bo's father's family. Bo also had depression. We are now both stable doing well and taking anti-depressants. We will both take them for the rest of our lives. There is no cure. The troubles with Bo didn't help but they didn't cause my depression. It was just bad luck, genetically

My parents have been happily married for more than sixty years. I had a fun and a white picket fence upbringing and was a happy teenager who didn't need drugs to get high. I was one of the lucky ones. I wasn't prepared for this world of drugs and alcohol. I used to think that marijuana was acceptable but now I think it's a gateway substance to harder and more dangerous drugs, especially if you have a predisposition toward addiction or mind-altering substances. Today many kids start with marijuana and move straight to heroin, which is very cheap. I count my blessings that Bo never used heroin, which is the toughest drug to quit.

If I can help one person or one family by sharing our story, then I am happy to talk about addiction. I don't want to be pitied and neither does Bo. Each day is a new one. I live each day one at a time and so does he. You just try putting one foot in front of the other.

—D'Arcy A.

Learning the Art of Grieving

People often say to me, "I could never survive the loss of a child." They said it to me when my 31-year-old son, Kenneth, died of AIDS, and seven years later when my 42-year-old daughter, Corinne, died of breast cancer. I now know that many people believe it is nearly impossible to survive the loss of a child and to live well afterwards.

As a therapist, having worked with scores of parents experiencing the loss of a child, I know death is not the only way to lose a child, perhaps not even the worst way. Parents can be asked to deal with a child becoming addicted to drugs, or seriously injured in an automobile accident, or while playing sports, being sent to prison, becoming ill with a serious mental or physical illness, or being shot in the street by friend, foe, or a police officer. And then there is the excruciating pain of the parent whose child harms or kills someone else.

In the short-term aftermath of Corinne's death, I visited my acupuncturist and mentioned my extreme tiredness. "It's not that I'm not hungry," I told him, "it's just that I'm often too tired to hold my fork." After the two-year journey accompanying

Corinne through her diagnosis and treatments, helping care for her three children, and being her caregiver the summer she underwent a bone marrow transplant, I was in a hypersensitive space.

"Grief takes your chi (life force)," was the acupuncturist's explanation. That seemed profoundly true, though not something I'd seen in the mental health literature on the stages and phases of the grief process.

I remembered experiencing that extreme tiredness before, seven years earlier, after Ken lost his battle with AIDS. His diagnosis had come at a time when AIDS was a death sentence, so for three and a half years, Ken courageously used meditation, complementary medicine regimes, and his love of music and the theater arts to stay healthy. He also participated in a medication trial for what became "the cocktail," all in the hope that he would be alive for the cure he knew to be just around the corner.

Ken inspired me throughout that process and continues to do so all these years since his passing. While I was waiting in the wings to dance at the celebration of his life, tears began to fill my eyes. Ken's voice in my head interrupted me and turned my tears to laughter. "You can cry tomorrow, Mom. It's Show Time!"

Research on resilience documents well the role of support in enabling people to get through their challenges and become stronger from having done so. But when Ken was diagnosed with AIDS in 1993, the stigma of the disease prevented him from telling anyone, not even his best friend, if he wanted to keep his job. As mental health professionals, my husband and

I had friends and colleagues we could trust for support but we knew the truth of what a Native American healer said in a presentation for AIDS caregivers, "A disease that is kept a secret cannot heal."

Five years after Ken died, when Corinne faced her death-defying challenge, the issue of breast cancer and finding a cure had broad community support. It was hard to buy a box of cereal or a bottle of shampoo that didn't have a pink ribbon on it. And Corinne was a magnet for people who wanted to help.

As we were going through the ups and downs of dealing with what my husband called, "the Big Suck," the love and service of friends, family, and communities of people held us up. Someone delivered a meal to Corinne's house four nights a week for two years. Someone shopped for birthday and Christmas presents and someone wrapped them. Ten-year-old Will's soccer team joined "Team Corinne" to Walk for the Cure. When a reporter asked the kids why they were walking they said, "Because Will is our friend."

People tell me I'm an expert on getting through tough stuff. Whether or not that's true, I've felt compelled to share what I've learned from my children and others through the experiences we had together. I saw this as a way to honor them and the gifts they gave in the midst of their own suffering. I was determined to become a good enough writer to tell the stories of what helped and what hindered, perhaps to ease other people's journeys, journeys more common than our culture wants to admit.

Expressive arts were important vehicles that helped me get through the challenges and I became intrigued to learn more about how art and creativity heal. Anna Freud and her famous father identified artistic creative expression as an example of what they called "sublimation"—channeling the unpleasant emotions and urges into socially acceptable ways. Turning to writing about these adversities, I deliberately went back into the experiences to ruminate on the details of what transpired: the good and the difficult, the bad and the beautiful. From this vantage point, it's been possible to gain new understandings, make connections and meaning, and identify creative solutions.

I gained and used tools to tell my stories by becoming involved in an art-based improvisational performance system during and since those times of extreme hardship. From singing my anger in the shower, to demonstrating it in my TEDx talk, to performing stories side by side with my husband, highlighting our different perspectives on the same situation, to writing an award-winning book and articles that share with others what I've learned—these all have moved me in the direction of post-traumatic growth and away from the post-traumatic stress, which is familiar to many people.

The enduring gifts from my grief's creative art making have profoundly changed me. I discovered that life is not lived in months, or years, days, or hours, but in moments. When we can bring ourselves fully into our moments, (which happens more often in times of extreme adversity), we enliven them and make them memorable and accessible.

My relationship with my children continues today as many moments from the tough times continue to inform my present and enlighten my future. When I broke my shoulder in a fall in my dance class, or a medical emergency caused me to have to take a most undesirable medicine, I remembered all that my children willingly endured in the hope of gaining more years of life. I stop complaining and focus, as they did, on living my life as fully as possible under the new circumstances.

Since many things that I deeply desired did *not* happen (like the cure of my children's diseases), yet other amazingly positive things *did,* I no longer expect the future to look like I imagine it, or planned for it, or to match what people around me expect.

A magnet on my refrigerator proclaims the message, "Let the butterflies come to you." When I can adopt this attitude of surrender, learned initially in the toughest of times, it seems to create more opportunities for surprise, delight, and a moment-by-moment appreciation for just being alive.

—**Sheila K. Collins**, PhD

Helping Others Overcome Loss

After my daughter passed away from heart disease, life was a struggle. I was a single mom and had to figure out life. After five years I have decided to go back to school to be a grief counselor to help others who are in a situation that I was once in. I want to be able to help them overcome the loss and pain and sympathize with them and know that I have been there and it gets better, even though there will be rough days. I look at it as my gift from God to pay it forward.

—**Amanda Warthen**

The Shared Bond of Bereavement

My husband passed away in 2012, leaving me with two daughters, ages sixteen and nineteen at the time. It was the most difficult time in my life, having to accept our new "normal" life and now rediscovering who I am.

I met my husband at age nineteen and lost him at age forty-eight. I really didn't know any other life without Phil. The whole part of creating a new life scared me tremendously as well as facing a future without my husband and the life we had was gone.

I turned to a local bereavement group a year after my husband died, one specifically for young widows and widowers on the same journey I was. I immediately connected with the others and formed long-lasting friendships with the bond we share as a base. I turned into the "group social director" planning dinners and events. Now I am helping the facilitators at our sessions without any formal training other than sharing my experiences in the process and believing my message will help the new members with hope, courage, and the ability to live again. My heart is open to help those who lost their spouses by giving them the tools to transition their lives from heartache to healing.

—Deidre Antonucci

Passing on Dad's Wisdom

My dad, my world, passed away on Thanksgiving Day when I was twelve. Thankfully, he taught me so much in those twelve years I had the strength to press on. He taught me to always strive for the best and to be kind to others. I didn't know it then, but he taught me to have an open heart and be ready for whatever challenges or opportunities might come. I used those lessons to become the first in my family to graduate college. I pass them on now to countless others as I work at a university advising college students.

—Lacey Ruminer

Trying to Save Even One Life

I always wanted to teach CPR but as a child I was abused by my stepfather. He told me that I was ugly and I would never amount to anything in life. I wanted to be loved and I wanted to achieve, and because of my situation growing up I became more determined to prove him wrong. The sad part was even when I achieved this I felt I was not worthy. On September 22, 1996, my youngest son committed suicide from depression after my first husband died in a car accident. He missed his father so much. He once told me, "Mom, I love you so much but I really miss dad terribly." This became my drive to make a difference in the lives of others. If I could save just one life or teach others to do this then my son would not have died in vain. I started teaching for Inspira Medical as a CPR instructor and decided this was not enough. I saved up for and bought mannequins and taught classes in my community for free. Teaching CPR helped me overcome my adversity by giving to others in a positive way. I opened my heart once again.

—Anonymous

A Journey of Loss and Restoration

My open heart formed through its painful breaking. As a mother, I know the incredible grief of losing my beautiful fifteen-year-old daughter to sarcoma cancer. Serving Leah through her fourteen-month illness impacted my life forever. While I grieve, I'm committed to helping others who also hurt. I support my daughter's teenage friends, help grant wishes in her memory, and write a blog that shares my journey of loss and restoration. I have been told that, by transparently opening my heart, my story encourages others to better understand their emotions, share their loss stories and move toward healing.

—Marie Guthrie

Part Four

The Strength of Children and Their Parents

Having children is an incredible gift. You bring them into this world and you love them unconditionally. The journey you expected changes when your children have mental or physical issues, but these challenges are another opportunity to help others on their journey. Loving your children unconditionally and helping them find their talents and strengths is priceless. As a mother of six, I know that they all have their own journey and the challenge is to hear them and support them through their choices.

Exceptional Minds for Exceptional Kids

One of the greatest challenges of my life has been raising a child with special needs. I had an exciting, successful career in the movie business—I'm a member of the Motion Picture Academy and the Directors Guild of America—and thought I would work in that field until retirement. My darling son, Noah, was born in 1994. For two years, he met the typical developmental milestones and although his language was slow to develop, he used about fifty words. At age two and a half, he suddenly stopped talking. It was shocking. This was in 1997—before the internet and the awareness of autism that exists now. We went from doctor to doctor and Noah was finally diagnosed with autism at age three. My husband (Bob Schneider) and I were devastated. During my pregnancy, we joked about what Ivy League college our son would attend; now we were wondering if he would be accepted into kindergarten.

I read the few books then available about autism and drove Noah to his therapies. My amazing husband did extensive research and kept me from falling apart. We bonded with a few other families in our area and decided that we would somehow survive by banding together and helping each other. From this group, Bob and I founded the Foothill Autism Alliance, a nonprofit dedicated to providing education, resources, and support to families with children on the autism spectrum. Life was difficult as Noah had sensory issues and very little language. He was isolated and frustrated, and he would weep when he could not communicate with us. Gradually, the therapies started helping but just when life had settled down a bit, my husband was diagnosed with lymphoma. Noah was only five. Tragically, Bob died three years later. I was suddenly a single mother of an autistic child and Noah, who had been extremely close with his father, was totally distraught. Somehow, I managed to run Foothill Autism Alliance for five years after Bob's death and happily, the organization continues to help families today.

Noah was gradually regaining language, but in middle school his development plateaued. At a friend's suggestion, I signed him up for an after-school animation class. The class turned out to be a game changer! Not only did Noah learn to make animated shorts, but his communication and engagement improved dramatically as did his schoolwork. He showed several of his shorts at his bar mitzvah—there wasn't a dry eye in the room! He started entering his films into competitions and won numerous awards. Watching Noah flourish in the animation classes, I began thinking about all the kids with autism who are amazingly talented but have nowhere to go after high school. With a group of like-minded parents, we formed a nonprofit in 2009 and opened Exceptional Minds (EM) in 2011. The school is a three-year vocational program to train students with autism to work in visual effects and animation. We were desperate parents looking for a way our children could have meaningful, independent lives. We started with nine students the first year; now we have students applying from all over the country and sadly, have to turn away potential candidates due to limitations of space and money. Today, we also offer summer programs and private and small group sessions so high school kids can try out the program.

The unemployment rate for people with autism is very high. Once they finish high school, there are few career paths available for young adults with autism. To help our graduates find work, we opened Exceptional Minds Studio (EMS) in 2014. Upon graduation, our artists are either placed in paid outside work or are employed by EMS, working on professional projects. Finding jobs for people with autism is difficult because we have to change many hearts and minds. When we place a graduate in a job, we work closely with the employer and provide job coaching to ensure success. Noah was in the third graduating class and worked in EMS for over a year. Now he is planning to return to art school and get a degree in fine arts or animation. He just got his driver's license...amazing given his journey!

I was director of operations at Exceptional Minds for six years and am now serving on their board of directors. I also actively volunteer with other nonprofits to create different kinds of jobs for people with autism. I want to share the experience I've had with Exceptional Minds. There is a great need for more programs; working together, we can change lives and make the world a better place!

—**Yudi Bennett**, exceptionalmindsstudio.org,
2017 Open Hearts Honoree

* * *

I got involved with Exceptional Minds five years ago when Yudi Bennett, one of the co-founders, asked me to help set up the school/studio and join the board of directors. When we were about to graduate our first class, I came aboard full-time as the VFX Producer and Job Developer to help set up and manage a professional visual effects studio for Exceptional Minds.

For more than twenty years, I had a very successful career in film production and then eventually became a VFX Producer. I won a Grammy Award for the music video "I'm Fat" starring Weird Al. When the opportunity to run the Exceptional Minds Studio came up, I knew it was the right move. I wanted to give back to these talented kids on the autism spectrum and use my skills in visual effects so they could become independent and accomplish something with their lives.

I was disadvantaged as a child and there were very few people around to help or inspire me. I was in orphanages (Jewish institutions where the kids were not allowed to be adopted since their parents were still alive) from age three to seventeen, and I was very unhappy as a child. My parents were not around to help me or support me growing up. I knew I would make a better life but I didn't know what it was. After I got my working papers, I was on my own and worked my way through college. I first got into theater as an assistant lighting designer in New York and then I moved to work in film, starting as a production assistant, location manager, production manager and then to visual effects. I had an incredible amount of success without parental guidance. I had to do a lot independently and learn from my mistakes. For two decades, I was very successful and well respected in the studio industry in spite of my personal struggles as a child growing up in New York.

I knew one day I would give back to artists or young adults. It is very rewarding to help others develop themselves professionally. There are so many disadvantaged kids. I want to show them that you can become something if you put your mind and heart toward it. I want to inspire others to do better in their lives and go after their dreams.

With the studio, the young adults are working and earning a paycheck. They have autism but they can function independently and have rewarding jobs.

I am now the Studio Executive Producer at Exceptional Minds Studio where we have three supervisors and eleven artists; we work on visual effects projects for major Hollywood studios. Initially, I used my connections in the industry to reach out to get small projects. When we completed those jobs, we started to prove ourselves and got repeat business for bigger projects.

We are the only school/studio in the U.S. that is teaching young people with autism to develop careers in visual effects and animation. We try to place at least half of our graduates in outside positions at either production companies or visual effects facilities and the rest work as artists in our studio. It is an amazing program and I am honored to be part of it. I wish that more businesses would train kids who are on the autism spectrum. Once they are trained, they are terrific workers. We look at the ability, not the disability and we hope we are inspiring other people to do the same.

—**Susan Zwerman**, exceptionalmindsstudio.org,
2017 Open Hearts Honoree

* * *

I was raised by a single mother and was the first one in my family to go to college. I became a visual artist and ran Merian Creative Studio. But when I was asked by Yudi—a determined single parent wanting to help her autistic son—I said I would help out. While still running my studio, I spent about ten hours teaching at Exceptional Minds. Gradually, those hours expanded because I was so enthralled with the kids. Some couldn't look me in the eye or shake my hand, and I had to explain they needed to do those things in a work environment.

It was time for me to do something from the heart, not involved with my clients. I hadn't worked with autistic kids so I didn't put limits on what they could do. I assumed they could do everything and they've met all my expectations. Over the past six years we've built something incredible at the studio.

—**Ernie Merian**, exceptionalminds.org,
2017 Open Hearts Honoree

Showing Endless Love to My Hero

Watching my son fight cancer from the age of five months old, I have an open heart of endless love and admiration for him. My mind and faith is endless as I watch him battle each day with a smile. He is my hero and I try to show him endless love every day to fight another day.

—**Lydia Carneson**

A Child's Smile

My great granddaughter can make me smile when the world is getting me down. My husband is going through cancer again, and this little charmer really helps to take our minds off personal tragedy and enjoy the moment at hand. We have custody of this little darling and will continue to fight the good fight because of her love. We cannot surrender to defeat. With open hearts and minds, we continue every day.

—Penny Sanders

Focus on What Can Be Done

When my son, Zachariah was four he was diagnosed with Asperger's syndrome. At first, I worried about all the things he might never do. I chose to focus on all his strengths instead and worked to make him believe he could do anything he wanted to. Today he is seventeen, captain of his high school swim team, and a straight A student with a lot of friends. Next year he will be going to college to pursue his dream of becoming a college professor. I believe anything is possible with an open heart and open mind.

—Amy Duncan

A Miracle and Blessing

My heart opened when I was twenty-one years old and gave birth to my beautiful daughter Brittany. Together we have helped open the hearts and minds of people about what having Down syndrome really means. Twenty-six years later, she is a true miracle and blessing to our family and everyone she meets. Because of Brittany, I am about to graduate with a bachelor's degree in Social Work so I may be able to help others who have a disability.

—Renee Stuck

Celebrate the Little Things

I'm a single mother of three children. My children are all very special to me and special in their own ways. Two of my three children have Asperger's. My twenty-year-old son also possesses a high IQ and a photographic memory. My youngest, who is twelve, is a special needs child with a seizure disorder, autism, and who requires a special diet.

After having my son, the oldest of my children, I had seven miscarriages. Since we didn't believe I could have another child, when my son was seven, I adopted my oldest daughter. Her mother had approached me during her pregnancy and asked whether I would adopt her baby.

A short while after the adoption, I got pregnant. After so many miscarriages, I didn't expect the pregnancy to last. But it did. From her birth, we knew she had problems. She never stopped screaming for her first two years and couldn't be comforted at all. The doctors said she would never speak or look at anyone in the eye or understand anything. She has proven them all wrong.

For nine years, we lived in North Dakota so I could work with adults with developmental difficulties. This gave me an extraordinary education that has helped a great deal. We moved back to Texas and as my son was aging out of his program, his counselor offered me a part-time job with Community Healthcore. The job has since turned into a full-time position with me helping parents with educational issues, navigating through the system, running support groups, and more.

My youngest daughter continues to have seizures despite procedures she's undergone to help ease them. This has to be one of the hardest challenges a parent endures: Seeing your child suffering and there's nothing you can do. But then I remember all these parents I've met and worked with who were just as scared as I was when I first heard about autism. I was told all the things that she would never do and what a terrible life she would have. I see the fear in all these parents. That's the reason for me to keep going. I have to keep reaching out and helping other people. I go to schools and provide parenting strategies and family rules based on what has worked with my children. If my kids hadn't had difficulties, I wouldn't be able to help all these people and I wouldn't be working. I love my job; this is what I was born to do. Every single day, I am blessed by the people and families with whom I work.

And every day, my youngest teaches me not to worry about the big stuff but to celebrate the little things. Pretty soon, there are so many little things that the big ones no longer matter.

—**Regina Larson**

One Day at a Time

Some days it's not easy. But even on the worst day, if you know what to do, there is hope. Such is the life of a mom who loves someone on the autism spectrum.

In 2006, I found out that one of my sons has autism. It's never easy to hear, and it certainly wasn't then. But what made it infinitely harder was the way I was told. Unfortunately, it is an experience all too common for parents. After numerous therapists and months and months trying to find out what was going on, the psychiatrist simply said, "I think this is autism," and then, just as quickly, ushered me out the door. No explanation. No indication of what it meant for my son or his future. No offer of help or suggestions about what to do next. Nothing.

I wish I could say that my experience was unique. But unfortunately, it's not. Today, one in sixty-eight children is diagnosed with autism. So many parents are simply given a diagnosis and handed the checkout paperwork. No support is given, no guidance is offered, and no recommendations are provided about where to turn next. It is devastating news made worse by the lack of any direction, support, or encouragement.

Before finally getting an answer, I took my son to three different therapists. None of them offered much help or support. As a parent, it is a nearly unendurable pain to know something is going on with your child and no one knows how to help. It's harder still when the problems are escalating at home and nothing seems to ease his obvious anxiety, or provide relief for your suffering child. Desperation is the best word to describe this predicament.

When I finally met Timothy J. Wahlberg, PhD, of the Prairie Clinic in Geneva, Illinois, within five minutes, everything changed. I released a breath that I hadn't even known I was holding. At last, we had found our path. While nothing could change the diagnosis, having answers to my questions and someone who could explain to me what was happening was a huge relief. Working with Dr. Wahlberg helped me piece together a plan that has brought us much success.

After months of seeing Dr. Wahlberg with my son, listening to the brief explanations of autism that he could share in the last five minutes of our therapy session, and watching the problems with my son begin to turn around, I knew I had found the answers I had sought.

As time progressed, I was honored to be part of the writing team for Dr. Wahlberg's book *Finding the Gray*, which was a deep and profound education for me about autism, and which provided the missing piece that helped my life work. For years, in response to living with undiagnosed autism in other family members, I had sought personal growth and serenity through a number of therapies and family groups, and now I had the practical pieces to add to the solid spiritual repertoire I had already created. Successfully living life with autism is very much about the inner game.

It was because of my experience—the confusion, uncertainty, and pain of not knowing how to find real help; the grief of having no answers; and the transformation we experienced—that I decided to create a support system for families faced with autism. My mission is to provide an online resource so parents better understand how the autism affects their child and the rest of the family, and how to create success in life in spite of the existence of the autism.

I know my experience can help others find the road to peace much more quickly than I did. That's why I published my book, *Autism & The Rest of Us: How to Maintain a Healthy, Functional and Satisfying Relationship with Someone on the Autism Spectrum,* in 2015. And it's also why I founded the National Autism Academy in 2016. I want to give other families a way to get immediate tactical support, uplifting encouragement, and a healthier way to live with autism, all wrapped in the care of someone who has been there too, and delivered to their living room.

The National Autism Academy helps families get a clear path and real answers. It reveals secrets that many don't know, from Dr. Wahlberg's twenty-five years of clinical experience, plus practical interventions, parenting tips, emotional support, and most of all—real answers. Because the information on the inner workings of autism and how it affects thinking and behavior can change how parents understand their child and therefore their relationship, my academy can help provide a path where none seemed to exist. With this added knowledge, parents can nurture and help their kids grow in new, exciting ways. By educating parents about all aspects of life with autism, their family life can be so much more successful. And that makes even a day that's not easy, one filled with hope.

—Jeanne Beard

Unconditional Love

My amazing son Matthew was born with cerebral palsy. He hopes and dreams like any normal person. He has an exceptional personality and accepts life as it comes. He knows no other life than in a wheelchair. My life has been blessed through his unconditional love for me and his many friends developed through his compassionate and caring ways. I can't imagine my life without Matthew and know that I would change nothing if I could as he would not be Matthew without his disability. Greater Love is nothing other than to unconditionally love and respect a person with disabilities.

—Dora Douglas

Part Five

Faith

Whether it is traditional religion or some other spiritual connection, faith in some higher power can carry people through impossible odds and severe emotional and physical pain. The expression of faith varies from culture and country but having a belief that something is greater than you can give you guidance, compassion, and a compass to carry you through the road ahead. And you can be comforted by like-minded people who listen, pray, and care for one another. The power of a community with a common purpose whether faith based or not can be a powerful source of strength.

Life Is Too Short

Because of living with an open mind, God was able to take two broken hearts who met in a hospital, and whose spouses died a week apart, to find new love in each other that neither of us could have ever imagined. He has taken us through losing our spouses a week apart to holding each other through the loss of a parent each, a child, two granddaughters, and a sister together. We have learned that life is too short and precious to hold grudges or allow negative reactions and unforgiveness into our lives. We are blessed to have each other.

—Peggy Kimbrell

I Am Here to Help Others

God has shown me the way through much adversity in life. When I was eighteen I gave birth to my son, and due to a doctor's error, he suffered a traumatic brain injury. I am also a two-time cancer survivor having beat Hodgkin's lymphoma and malignant melanoma. I continue to keep my strong faith in God and I know He's kept me on earth to help others. I work in behavioral health helping people with mental illness. My dedication is to my God, my children, my family, and those I serve at work. I wouldn't change my path!

—Korina Candela

The Power of Prayer and Positive Thinking

I am fifty-six years young and I feel like God has a plan bigger than my imagination because of what He has brought me through in my lifetime thus far! From the travesty of molestation at the ages of seven and nine, to the loss of my fiancé in a terrible automobile accident at the age of eighteen, and being raped by two men in the same year...I am alive and well with two amazing sons, two beautiful daughters-in-law, and two adorable grandchildren! Thank God and the power of prayer and positive thinking! I love life!

—Cilinda Bogk

Lighten Your Own Burden

Battling through cancer has taught me what is important in this world: others in our life, those in our family and everyday lives, and those we meet on the journey. I don't want to waste a moment more of this life by judging, hating, or obsessing about things that aren't important. I make it my purpose to be there for others, whether stranger or friend—with a hug, a smile, a word of kindness, and a listening and loving heart. My own burden has become lighter and my own journey full of joy as a result.

—Maureen Hannan

A Small Group of Strangers Became Family

My husband and I grew up in homes that were somewhat dysfunctional. His father was an army sergeant who was very stern with his children, showing practically no love. Mine was a fatherless home and my older brothers went their own ways, leaving me feeling very much alone with my widowed mother.

As a result, both my husband and I had built "walls" around our hearts to keep the "world" from inflicting more hurt. That feels safe, but in effect, it brings isolation and loneliness.

We married and had two children, but we didn't really have friends. Our world consisted of work and home. But we saw ourselves repeating generational mistakes with our own two sons.

That all changed fifteen years ago when we made the decision to become a part of the large, wonderful church where we now worship and serve. When we first became members, they had just started a program called "Cell Groups." These were small groups that would meet once a week in the home of the leader or one of the members. It would involve fellowship with each other, refreshments, a short Bible lesson, and then we would pray for one another's needs.

Well, we joined a group that met in our area, and from the very first night, we felt like we had come home! Those wonderful people took us in and showered us with love and affection. We felt accepted and "liked," more than either of us ever had in our lives.

That group became the family both of us had yearned for! It was a combination of men and women, some of the "older" generation, some younger, African American, white, a family from Trinidad, single, married, divorced, or widowed. The group had about thirty members and we met each week for almost three years.

They prayed us through some very bad times when my husband lost his job and was unemployed for quite a while. They prayed for us and loved us through sicknesses and injuries, through the death of one of my husband's brothers, and other tragedies—and we prayed for and cared about them as well. We came to depend upon our "family" in that group, and when we saw them at church, it was like seeing a brother, a sister, a parent, or a grandparent. We knew we were loved.

The leader of the group, a wonderful woman named Norma, became a surrogate mother to me and taught me how to live as a Godly woman. She taught me how to love people, how to forgive those who hurt you, how to be a blessing to others, and how to be a better parent. Several of the men were just as much a blessing to my husband. Knowing these people truly changed our lives—changed us as people.

Though Norma had to step down as leader due to circumstances in her own life, and the members moved on to other groups, we all still see each other from time to time and that bond is still felt, even after twelve years.

It was a precious time in our lives and we thank God for it, and for those wonderful people who opened their hearts to us and loved us unconditionally.

—Linda Bullock

A Cinderella Story

As a child, how many of you wanted *to be* that romantic character? Maybe you envisioned your life would be like that of a hero or heroine you dreamed about, perhaps in a movie or TV show. What about you? Who did you want to be or who did you look up to?

As a young girl, I absolutely loved Cinderella. Well, actually, Cinderella *and* her dress that she wore to the ball. As a child, that was the most beautiful dress I had ever seen with all the sparkles and flowing yards of blue satin material, which shimmered when she turned in any direction. Then of course, you can't forget the glass high-heeled slippers that instantly turned her feet into a thing of beauty. Even now, when I look at that image it invokes in me dreams of love and fairytale endings. It is the moment that little girls daydream about: finding a handsome man who will ride in like Prince Charming and the two of you can ride off into the sunset to live happily ever after with you as his Princess.

As children, we all want that sense of identity; to be that special someone to somebody. I know I did. With my dream firmly in my mind, I began my journey. At age eighteen, I entered the Army. I meet a man right away and we started dating. Before I knew it, he asked me to marry him and I accepted. He took me to the jewelry story and told me to pick out a ring!

That wasn't the picture I had imagined but off to the altar we went. I was age twenty and he was twenty-three. Three months later, I became pregnant, and three months after that he had his first affair. As you might have guessed, our marriage ended in divorce. Our thirteen years of marriage were bookended with his adulteries and, adding even more drama to the already stressful situation, pornography addiction throughout.

When that happened, I felt like my identity was destroyed, particularly because of the betrayal and rejection that had occurred year after year. I found myself a single woman facing the daunting task of raising my five children alone. At the time of the separation, the children's ages were one, four, six, eight, and eleven. I remember talking to God about this situation. I reminded him that I did *not* sign up to raise these kids alone and He needed to remedy the situation as quickly as He could! I was not a happy camper, and I stomped my foot and told God so. Well, funny thing about God, He does not move us out of a particular situation until we become content with where we are. And in order for me to be content, all I had to do was ask and God would give me the strength to get there.

God wanted me to learn to be content, no matter what, single or married. When I became content in the situation I was in, as a single mother with five small children, and when I surrendered my will to His, he was then able to quietly say, "Ok, *now* you are ready, now you can have your heart's desire."

At the age of thirty-five, my Prince Charming arrived and swept me off my feet. I truly fell in love for the first time in my life and I was loved by a man for the first time in my life. He was a Christian man who wanted to serve God every bit as much as I did. It was a dream comes true. We were both pastors' kids, loved music, loved to travel, wanted to serve the Lord in church and in ministry, and we were both business-minded yet loved to laugh together and live life to the fullest. It was truly a match made in Heaven, and we often said that we were God's gifts to each other. Both of us had experienced the betrayal and rejection of a spouse and never wanted to experience that again. This was that second chance that we had always heard about and, in the secret places of our minds, dreamed about.

We threw ourselves into loving each other and our blended family of now seven children ranging from ages four to fourteen. We had our share of tough times with the children so we planned a couple of vacations a year by ourselves. It was always a much-needed time of regrouping and bonding. Life was good. We were in ministry together as Sunday school teachers and he was a worship leader while I sang with the Praise Band. We would occasionally have heated discussions about the discipline of the children and a few other minor issues but other than that, things were pretty peaceful. We got along with many moments of laughter to lighten the atmosphere and we worked hard building his business. The finish line of becoming "empty-nesters" was in sight! To be honest, we day dreamed about that—just a tiny bit—although we would never trade our family for the world. On the nights when we got to sit around the dinner table together or have a Thanksgiving meal as a family, we would look at them sitting around the table and *know* it was *so worth it*!

I will never forget a particular day in November, November 20, 2015, to be exact, my husband and I had just left a business meeting. I had been feeling a little uneasy and I asked him if we could talk for a minute. It was a little chilly out and because we drove two cars I asked him if we could talk in his truck. We jumped in, he turned on the heater then I turned to him and asked, "Honey, you seem off, are you tired, are you okay? Are we okay? What is wrong?

He replied, "I need a break from you and the kids."

Stunned I just stared at him. I asked him to clarify by asking what exactly he meant by "a break."

He buried his head in his hands, rubbed his face and said, "I don't know."

I asked again, "A break, you need a break, what kind of break exactly?"

He responded again saying, "I don't know."

In shock I asked again, "A break, as in divorce?" He responded once again with, "I don't know."

I couldn't think, I couldn't breathe, and all I knew was that I had to get out of that truck before I would break down and wail in pain and anguish. I scrambled to find the latch on the door and flung myself out of his truck. I said, "You want a break, then go," and slammed the door behind me and darted to my car before he could see the gushing tears now coming from my eyes. I got in my car, fumbling to find the keys to start the car. I remember thinking that this couldn't be happening to me again. "Oh no, not again, I loved my husband, life was good, what was happening" I cried out in the privacy of my car. Once again, my identity was crushed and my world came crashing down around me. This time was totally different from the first time. The last time, I was fearful but relieved. In the previous marriage, I was tired of the abuse, the disdain, the disrespect, the tests to make sure I did not have a venereal disease, the anger, the fighting, and the never-ending daily task to "make myself a better person so he would just love me." This time, I was staring at the man I loved and who I knew loved me just as deeply; my business partner, my best friend, my soul mate, the one I identified with. I was "Kevin's wife" and proud of it. Proud to stand by him and serve the God we loved and to raise our beautiful children. I could never imagine life without him. I had never even considered it!

Fast forward about eight months later, it was apparent my husband was not coming home. I found myself in a place I had never been before and I again asked God the question, "WHY?" I asked and God lovingly showed me another part of the why: my identity should never be placed in a man, in being a man's wife, or in a job, which for me meant being a successful real estate agent. My identity is not in a title the world can give me whether in business, church, or in the family. My identity was and always will be in Jesus Christ. I forgot that, and because I placed my identity in another person, when he failed me, I was lost. God was teaching me that my faith and identity is in Him. I have learned that God wants me to be *his* Princess, and *his* alone. That does not mean I cannot have a man's love or not be treated like a princess but God does not want me to ever let someone else take His place. I let my husband take God's place and placed my identity in him. My value and self-worth has been given to me by God, I am *his* princess, His child, not because of the man I married.

That was a lesson that I needed to learn. It was a valuable lesson but it was not enjoyable. God *does* allow for free will and bad things will occur to all of us.

We may never fully understand the *situational* why but we can always know the why we have been created.

We were created for God. He *WANTED* us. He wanted children, I imagine much in the same way we all want children. He loves us for who we are. We do not have to be or do anything to gain that status except reach out and accept His love. His unconditional love is gifted to us by the power of Jesus Christ through His death, burial, and resurrection. When we believe in Jesus Christ and that God raised Him from the dead that automatically makes us His Prince and Princess. Our identity is then in Him, and Him alone.

All royalty wear a crown to symbolize who they are. Imagine, for a moment, that at night, we take off our spiritual crowns and place them on the bedside table. Then, as the light of day dawns, I venture a guess that *many* of us forget to place that crown back on our heads. That crown is a reminder to us and to the world of who we are in Jesus Christ!

If you have surrendered your will to Jesus Christ, remember your identity is in Him, that you are a Prince or a Princess, right along with me. So every morning, stand up straight, pick up your crown, adjust it high on your head, and go into the world *acting* like the Prince or Princess that God created you to be!

—Valerie Sullivan

There's No Blood Between Us
Except the Blood of Jesus

In 2010, one of my best friends suffered a subarachnoid hemorrhage several months after giving birth to her fourth child. I had been blessed to be in the delivery room when the baby was born and even shot the video (although I am sure it was not done well because my excitement held my ability to video hostage that day). That morning when I received the phone that Lisa was in ICU in an Atlanta hospital and it "did not look good," my heart hit the floor.

My parents both passed away years before this so I was no stranger to loss. But this was one of my best friends. She and I had so many things in common that we considered ourselves sisters. We homeschooled our children together and went to church together. We were not simply friends. We were family. As soon as I could, I jumped in the car and headed down to the hospital. I drove like a madwoman on the highway, listening to worship music, and screaming and crying to the Lord for him to please spare her life. She had a brand-new baby and three other children who needed her and a husband whose life would be destroyed if she didn't make it.

The look on everyone's faces told me that her chances were slim. However, when I spoke to her husband and he said that the doctors said most people do not even make it to the hospital after suffering a subarachnoid hemorrhage, that was all the fuel I needed for my fire of hope. I went in to see her and, I'll be honest, it as the scariest thing I had ever seen—a young, vibrant woman connected to all those tubes, sedated, appearing lifeless. But I held her hand and talked to her about how she had to come back because we all needed her. When I left her room that day and later traveled on the highway to my house, I gave her over to the Lord. I wanted her to be with us but I wanted my friend—my sister—and if I could not have her back the way she was before, then I was willing to let her go.

The next day, I went back and found out she was awake! She wanted to see me! I immediately went in and was able to talk to her. She wanted to know if she had died, and was she going to live. We had the most special chat I've ever had with anyone. Together we cried and believed that all would be well. Within the week, she was out of ICU, which had allowed me to stay over at night with her in the hospital. We had a night full of laughs because her memory was terrible and she asked the same questions a hundred times. We sang worship songs and when she couldn't remember any others, she sang "Dancing Queen" by ABBA—because God was the Abba Father. When her lower back and legs ached, I was honored to massage them for her and we laughed at the awkwardness of our positions. That night, we bonded in a way that I will never forget. Previously, I had thought the birth of a child was the ultimate bonding. Not so! Of course, Lisa does not even remember that night! But it was a night that sealed our friendship in my heart and made us more than friends. We became family.

You don't get to choose your family but you can choose your friends. However, I believe that some friends are chosen for us because they are meant to be family. Seeing the miracle of life in the delivery room with Lisa and then again in the hospital with her and at home in the following weeks changed my views on friendship and the importance of having it. Taking a road trip with her several months later was the ultimate blessing. When you find a friend that feels like family, it is one of the most awesome gifts you can ever receive.

—Anonymous

With God's Help

I was eleven years old when I was involved in a fishing accident that left me blind for six months in my left eye; I needed five surgeries to restore my eyesight. My brother was learning to cast and the hook went in my left eye. I faced ridicule from my peers at school. It is a miracle I still have my eye! Growing up is hard and I faced a lot of challenges. I chose to be positive and have faith that God would help me through. My parents were there by my side through it all. That experience allowed me to have an open heart not to give up, as well as a strong desire to help people. Once I grew up I joined the Saint Vincent de Paul Society at my church. We volunteer to help families and individuals in emergency situations. My experience taught me that no matter what we go through, if you love others and yourself, you will see it through. Sometimes bad things happen to show you where you're meant to go to help others. I devote my spare time and career to helping others.

—Anonymous

Sisters Through an Orphanage

In 2005, I was asked to join a group of women from my church to spend a week in an orphanage in Reynosa, Mexico. I was reluctant at first but I decided to go. That decision has changed my life. Not only have I become involved with the children at the orphanage (returning several times) but in the years since I have become extremely close with several of the women. Even though we see each other at church we still meet or talk during the week and enjoy weekends together at the Jersey shore. These women are the "sisters" I never had, and they have been my lifeline so many times over the past few years. I know I can count on them at any time (and have) to help me through the many struggles I've recently had in my life. They are always there for me. And likewise, as they have done for me, I would do for them. They are an extension of my biological family that I will always cherish. I bless each one of them and thank God that He brought them into my life.

—Jeanne Sico

Love Is the Best Christmas Present

When I was age seven, my dad lost his corporate job. A few years before he was cut, his company transferred him and his family of six kids from Florida to a small town on the outskirts of Atlanta.

After he lost his job, my parents began managing a 20-room motel there in Northwest Georgia. Family living quarters came as a benefit of working there, so my sisters, brothers, and I were able to watch many a character check in and out of the motel.

A few days before Christmas that year, my dad called a family meeting. He told us we would draw names from a hat for gift-giving. I had never drawn names before, but I thought it sounded fun. He said he would give each of us $5 to spend on the family member whose name we drew.

I drew the name of my older sister, Karin. She was eighteen. With all the naïveté of childhood, at age seven, I took my money and went to our small town square to Christmas shop.

My first stop was the jewelry store. I realize now how ridiculous it was to shop in a jewelry store with a $5 bill. Nevertheless, I went inside and quickly found the perfect gift for my sister. It was a blue and gold medallion on a large gold chain that cost $2.50. I knew my sister would love it.

My next stop was the dime store. I examined row after row of lip gloss, rubber balls, and sets of colored construction paper. I finally chose a large sew-on patch of a bunch of grapes. I don't remember what I paid for it, but I had finished my Christmas shopping. I had two treasures for my sister.

My dad drew my name. I'm sure I got a toy or two that Christmas, but what I remember most is a present he made—a book of songs he wrote and illustrated for me.

My two-year-old daughter, Hayden, and I visited my parents at their home recently. When Hayden dug through a jewelry box my mom set out for her, one of the first pieces she pulled from it was the old medallion. My mom had found it and kept it all these years.

I found the song book, too, in a box of old family pictures stored at my house. My dad included blank paper after his compositions for me to write songs of my own. I laughed as I read the songs I wrote at age seven.

My family moved back to Florida a few years after living in the motel, and my dad worked other corporate jobs and started several businesses. Our Christmases were different after that. We never drew names again. I never received another song book. It's funny to me now that the song book and the medallion made it through all our family moves and life changes.

"I couldn't believe you gave me that medallion," my sister, Karin said when I called her the other day. "It was so beautiful. You probably don't remember, but I wore that. It was a real present," she added.

I think we all got real presents that year.

Even though some ads try to pressure us into buying last-minute Christmas gifts or stocking stuffers, they can't offer deals on love.

All I have to do is remember a Christmas I spent in a Georgia motel years ago to know love outlasts any gadget or toy.

And love is the best Christmas present any of us can give or receive.

—Nancy Lee Bethea

God's Joy

My mother wore deep red lipstick on her large, beautiful lips. I grew up watching that vibrant mouth constantly smile-in-the-midst of whatever was happening to her. So that's what I did too. I smiled. I accepted and kept a lot of things inside me when circumstances were difficult and disappointing, unfair, and sad.

My father was a workaholic and only gave me attention when I did what he wanted and worked hard. So that's what I did.

I overachieved, smiled, looked pretty, and performed my way through things like my parents' divorce, my mother stealing us kids in the middle of the night, moving from our home in Hawaii to Oklahoma, abandonment, financial challenges, and lots of health issues. While I accepted these facts, I started telling myself things like, "I'm not as good as everyone else; I'm ugly, no one notices me; I'm not important." But I hoped and prayed things would get better.

In college, I chose a high-profile career as a TV news reporter and anchor where I could look good, ask questions, and never had to reveal anything personal. When I scored a position as the Dallas reporter for *Entertainment Tonight*, I felt I was finally on my way to a happy, fulfilled life.

But then my mother died from cancer on my twenty-eighth birthday. She had been the only person I ever felt love from. My first daughter also almost died as she was diagnosed with a serious kidney disease, experienced profound hearing loss, and severe scoliosis. For her first eighteen years, Children's

Hospital was our second home. While I accepted these facts, inside I told myself things like, "Kalli's health complications are my fault; I'm a loser; I'm not a good parent; I don't know what to do." But, I hoped and prayed things would get better.

Shortly after my fortieth birthday, I was diagnosed with a rare cancer. Doctors said if I didn't immediately begin chemotherapy, radiation, and then have surgery, I could die within two weeks. So, I began therapy and had surgery to chop off the lower part of my backbone.

Just a few years after shining brightly in television news, I was in agony in a hospital bed, barely able to move. The next ten years were filled with severe complications including yearly emergency surgeries (including removing my colon), frequent hospitalizations, infections, and blockages. I was forced to rely on friends and family for basic care. My two daughters, ages two and five when I was diagnosed, lived with the reality that mommy could die any day.

While I accepted all these unending negative circumstances, my internal self-talk entertained thoughts like, "I'm getting worse. Another complication is around the corner. I'll never be strong. I'm about to die. I can't take this pain any longer. I'm afraid. I'm so depressed." But on the outside, I kept trying to smile while hoping and praying things would get better.

They didn't. After ten tough years of medical complications, life's stress and challenges took their toll on my marriage and sadly, my husband and I divorced. My daughters and I were homeless for a time and our financial challenges became even more severe. It was difficult to smile through this reality but I was so accustomed to passively accepting whatever came my way that I kept my pain hidden, trying to look like I was happy and content.

By the grace of God, the constant health complications paused for a few years. I began working part-time trying to rebuild life for my daughters and myself. Things slowly began looking up. Finally, I thought, my situation was changing and my prayers were being answered.

Then, I was diagnosed with exactly the same cancer.

A large cancerous tumor was present and cancer was spreading through my lymph system. My head began swirling, as I began hearing the equivalent of a loudspeaker playing a death march.

Liza, this time, you're going to die. You're all alone. You don't even have anyone to help you. You can't afford to treat cancer. You are such a burden. Just give up now. You're going to ruin Kalli's and Kate's lives *again!*"

As I walked out of my doctor's office listening to these toxic thoughts, I realized I needed to listen to something else or I would easily get lost in the confusion again and either go through years of living with fear of horrible medical complications again, or I would just die.

Thankfully, I had recently been studying scriptures in the Bible that describe how to experience transformation. I longed to transform from where I was into an authentic, strong, joyful woman on my outside and my inside.

Romans 12:2 says we can be transformed by renewing our minds. So that's what I was trying to understand. To renew my mind means I fill it with only things God would think. If

He wouldn't think something, then I shouldn't think about it either. *That* is the key to a renewed mind!

I knew this was a moment that would change my future. Listening to these lies was powerful enough to ruin my family and block my joy, forever affecting my children and their future children. I knew focusing on these beliefs could shut down the abundant life I had been walking towards. I knew that in this moment, the choice I made would affect my health, my family, my relationships, my joy, my peace, my strength, and the rest of my days here on earth.

So right there, spontaneously, as I walked to my car, I began talking to myself out loud. I declared, "NO! I refuse to listen to these thoughts and lies that are trying to take me down." I began replacing them with things I knew God thinks about and words He has said. Things like, "God gives me life so I have life! God's joy is my strength. God says He heals all my diseases, so thank you God, that you are healing me. I can do all things through You, who gives me strength. And, even though I'm feeling fear right now, I know fear doesn't come from You, so I declare, I am not afraid.

I intentionally walked strong as I tried to believe what I was telling myself out loud. I knew that people were staring at me as I talked to myself but I didn't care. I wasn't willing to limp like a cripple any longer. I could do something to stop the poison.

Once I reached my car, I climbed inside and slumped over. I sighed deeply through the sobs and reached my arms up in confusion. Was I doing this right? Could this really help me transform? It sure didn't feel like it. In fact, I felt like I was ignoring reality. Here I was—declaring that I was healed, strong, and joyful and yet, I could feel a large tumor on my body. So, I cried out to God. "Am I doing this right? This feels strange! Tests show I have a rare cancer, yet I'm saying I'm healed. God, this is awkward."

And then, I heard a voice that changed my life. It wasn't an audible voice. It was like a gentle impression in my heart. "Liza, there is TRUTH and there is FACT. Yes, cancer has been detected. That is FACT. But My Word says you are healed, strong, and joyful. That is TRUTH. I want you to focus on My Truth. I'll take care of the facts!"

Wow! It felt like a warm, safe, comforting hug from a Father who genuinely cares about his fragile daughter. As I allowed myself to receive God's Love and continued replacing the lies, facts, and negativity with His Truth, I knew this was the starting point of my life's greatest healing.

Today, I *am* transformed. Implementing this process every single day has changed my experience through another bout with cancer and it has also improved the outcome. With fear in the rearview mirror I am filled with unstoppable strength, joy, peace, and love no matter what I'm going through.

My passion is now helping others experience this kind of wholeness through their specific circumstances. At first, I came alongside friends and acquaintances who wanted what I had discovered. But as more of us began joyfully walking in our authentic identities, others began asking for help. So now I make myself available! I speak, coach people, and am writing a book that inspires and equips others to experience their own full, abundant lives.

These days, when a friend or client faces a difficult circumstance, instead of just praying and hoping the situation will change we take action. We open our hearts to receive God's love and we focus more on what He says about our circumstance. We don't ignore what's going on. We just pay more attention to God's Truth. God's Truth trumps fact. And *that* is transforming all of us into whole, strong, joyful, hopeful, and authentic expressions of ourselves.

—Liza Frampton

God Loves Everyone

I had the privilege of being raised in a home where love flowed freely, not just with each other, but to whoever needed it. My family moved around a lot when I was younger, but from my earliest memories until age ten, we lived in Pennsylvania. My dad was the pastor of a small community church that consisted of approximately thirty-five to forty families. We were all transplants; therefore, extended family was very limited. We became our own family, sharing all major holidays together as a church body. New Year's Eve, Memorial Day, and Labor Day were filled with game nights in the winter and picnics in the summer, but always fun and fellowship. Following Easter sunrise service the men would cook an all-church pancake breakfast for the women and children and then we would have the traditional service. We never knew who was going to join us for Thanksgiving dinner or if we would be babysitting for a church member on any particular night of the week. I have many fantastic memories from that time in my life and I always thought that was how life was supposed to be lived.

The experiences that I internalized during that first decade really shaped who I am today. Despite moving frequently since my early years, I have been blessed to have been adopted by a family everywhere I go. Even though I haven't lived in New Jersey for twenty-five years, I still have family living there today. My children have been fortunate enough to have met and experienced some of the love that incredible "family" showed me years ago. By learning at such an early age to be open to people from different backgrounds, experiences, and cultures, I feel I am able to be more accepting than I might have otherwise been. I also feel that God has blessed my openness by bringing some really rich friendships/extended family relationships into my life.

I, in turn, then am able to take the love that was poured into me from an early age and pass on that tradition by pouring it into the hearts and lives of the friendships I have acquired today, not to mention passing along the tradition of "adopted family" to my children. When I ran a daycare in my home for a number of years, the children I watched were not just a paycheck, they became family. A stranger on the street could not tell apart my biological children from the children I was blessed to help raise a certain number of hours per week. In addition, my children's friends are embraced as family when they walk through our door as well. My family has grown over the years through email connections, reconnected friend-ships, and even with cashiers at stores we frequent regularly.

Yes, I am very blessed to have been raised to embrace others, welcoming them into my circle of love. I pray that as a family we continue to bless those who are lonely, giving them a glimpse of the love God offers to everyone. I know that by giving of myself, I receive joy through each interaction. When I allow my heart to open wide, welcoming others, I find that family comes in many different varieties. If the world as a whole would take the same view, maybe one day we could all look on each other as family instead of strangers.

—**Anonymous**

Part Six

From Suffering to a Cause

Enduring the loss of a child or adjusting to limited physical mobility after an accident are unimaginable experiences. Even more incredible are people coping with the unthinkable who accept their circumstances and find a path ahead, not only to help themselves but others as well. These individuals could have remained "stuck" and isolated but they chose to move on, sometimes with grand formal plans to help others in similar situations, and in other cases, by simply being willing to talk about themselves and their struggles. Christopher Reeve has been a great inspiration for me as he was such a close friend, and I've come to know many remarkable young people who live life as fully as they can with the abilities they still have.

Random Acts of Kindness

When our middle daughter, Kayla, was barely seven years old, she was diagnosed with a rare form of brain cancer. For more than five years, we tried to walk a fine line between celebrating every day and going about our everyday lives. While this disease did not define Kayla, it did eventually tear her from our grasps. We will never fill the void that was created by losing Kayla, but every day we feel the love and the support of friends, family, neighbors, co-workers, and many others. When she passed away in our loving arms, she left us in the arms of so many people who knew and loved her—and of those who read about Kayla and were inspired by her story. Our hearts are warmed by the memories of the time that we spent together and of the random acts of kindness that are being performed in her memory. We are also greatly comforted by the surprising discovery that in leaving us, Kayla somehow made our family larger, not smaller.

At the time of her diagnosis, my wife, Laurie, and I were intensely private people who had no interest in sharing with friends and family, much less complete strangers, the innermost details of our family life. People deal with tragic circumstances and difficult challenges in different ways. Some reasonably decide to turn inwards. We, however, quickly discovered that there were tremendous stores of love in the bonds we had formed with those around us. We drew upon those reserves throughout the ordeal of first worrying about Kayla, then of trying to carry in the face of her disease, and finally of picking up the pieces after she was gone from our lives.

Over these many years, I have written detailed accounts of my interactions with Kayla. I began the process of writing about Kayla for a number of reasons. First, because she was so quiet and shy at the age of seven that she could not look an adult in the eye. Over time, her shyness disappeared as her treatments required her to become comfortable advocating for her needs and wants with doctors and nurses. Back then, however, her shyness made me worry that nobody would know how vibrant, brilliant, and funny she was. I was very afraid that she would seem to the world like nothing more than a victim of a tragic disease.

I also wanted to draw people into caring about Kayla and loving her the way we did. In part, I did that by sharing stories about Kayla's life and the ups and downs of her medical situation. In the process, Laurie and I did far more than develop an empathetic audience for Kayla. We developed a tightly knit, and yet widely expansive, network of friends and family to support us through this ordeal.

Living with—and eventually losing—Kayla taught us a great deal about living life to the fullest. We've shed tears to be sure. We've also had many laughs. We learned by watching Kayla's determination to live a normal life that we all possess tremendous power to overcome adversity. And we learned the power of family—both the family you are born with and the family that you make by opening your hearts to those who surround you.

—**Eric A. Wenger**, Kisses4Kayla.org

Keeping My Daughter's Dream Alive

Imagine you have one daughter and she had already survived neuroblastoma, a deadly form of pediatric cancer, when she was a toddler, and then the worst happens. Andréa, my daughter, was killed by a drunk driver at age twenty-four. I didn't think that I could go on. I envisioned closing the blinds and staying in bed. I always thought my main purpose in life was to be a mother. Now I was floundering because I was no longer a mother, and that feeling was devastating. At the same time, I was in the midst of a divorce after twenty-six years of marriage and leaving my home where Andréa had been raised. My life had been shattered.

It was (and still is) important for me to be able to talk about Andréa and listen to friends and families tell their stories about her. I had to let them know that it was okay for them to say her name and that I wouldn't cry. Hearing her name was a source of comfort because I knew she wasn't forgotten—which was my greatest fear.

About a month after my daughter's death, I got a note from one of her colleagues which read, in part, "Why don't we start a foundation and bring dance therapy to children who survived cancer or have learning disabilities?" This note immediately gave me purpose; Andréa was a special-education teacher and lifelong dancer who was passionate about helping children. She wanted to become a dance therapist. She also had learning disabilities as a result of her cancer treatments and knew firsthand the impact dance had on her full recovery, mentally and physically.

I grabbed onto the concept of this foundation. After you lose a child, especially so unexpectedly, there is no way to make things better but this was my chance to give meaning to my life and to honor hers. I wanted to make sense of my loss and find some way to accept that I had to go on without her. Although my daughter wasn't here, her dream would be alive. And through my darkest moments that first year after Andréa's death, I thought this foundation was a way for us to remain a team.

The bond between a parent and a child is always special but it is particularly strong when the child has survived cancer. I never left Andréa's bedside during the horrible, painful treatments she endured as a baby. We were so close and this foundation would help me to remain close to Andréa and her dream. I could accomplish something that she had wanted to do; this gave me purpose and meaning, which I desperately needed.

I was a teacher; I wasn't experienced or knowledgeable about raising money or running a nonprofit. But I believe if you are putting something positive into the universe, you will receive a lot of positive energy back. It was miraculous how things fell into place and people (including Jane Seymour) came into my life.

Several of Andréa's friends had been with me since her death. They planned the memorial service, attended hearings at the trial for the drunk driver, and they had great ideas for the Andréa Rizzo Foundation. One of them created a website. Another one designed our first brochure. I was teaching at the same elementary school Andréa had attended so I was surrounded by incredibly nurturing people who had watched Andréa grow up. They supported me and also offered amazing ideas for fundraising. Rather than feeling helpless, all of this compassionate effort gave me and my extended family a way to focus on the positive aspects of Andréa's life—and not the crushing weight of her death.

We needed to figure out how to make dance therapy a reality. I called one of my daughter's professors at NYU and learned that this service is usually provided in hospitals and schools. That gave me added inspiration because I knew that Memorial Sloan-Kettering was the place that Andréa herself wanted to give back to since she had been cured and given a second chance at life there. Somehow, I got to the right person at the hospital and wrote a mission statement, again with the help of several of Andréa's friends.

All of a sudden, I was surrounded by positive energy emanating from friends and family who wanted to make Andréa's dream come true too. I was introduced to a family in Rhode Island who also lost a daughter to a drunk driver; they met with me and taught me the ropes of setting up a nonprofit. Someone else recommended a lawyer and accountant. My father helped me tackle the paperwork for the 501(c)(3).

The Andréa Rizzo Foundation funds Dréa's Dream pediatric dance therapy program for children with cancer and special needs in hospitals and schools around the country. The program at Sloan Kettering serves as our flagship; it is the largest dance therapy program for kids with cancer. We also have programs at nine other sites around the country. Jane Seymour was instrumental in the foundation's growth.

She had donated one of her original Open Heart paintings, which we auctioned off to cover the airfare to send a child and a parent to a taping of *Dancing with the Stars*. We ended up being featured on several news programs; I met Jane and then met judge Carrie Anne Inaba who asked about the foundation and eventually became our national celebrity spokesperson. Jane Seymour was so warm and gracious; she featured Dréa's Dream on the Open Hearts website, a year before and a year later I was chosen as a winner of the Open Hearts Award and honored at the first annual Open Hearts gala. She made me feel that I was part of the Open Hearts family but more importantly, she acknowledged that the foundation was doing really important work. Getting that validation meant a great deal to me since I was learning as I went along—sometimes wondering if my ideas would actually work.

I am so fortunate that I don't have to ask people for money, my least favorite part of running a nonprofit. Our biggest supporters are young dancers who seek out our cause and voluntarily hold fundraising events throughout the year at universities and dance schools. Their work has been a gift on so many levels. I've developed close relationships with many of these volunteers, from the young women to the college students, as well as the dance school owners. They're so enthusiastic about my work and some of the students have gone on to become dance therapists after being inspired by Dréa's Dream.

I never imagined that I would experience joy again, but the Andréa Rizzo Foundation has brought both joy and excitement back into my life—a life that has been transformed from tragedy to triumph. I knew that our work was important and worthwhile, not only to the children and families we help, but it was Jane's support that helped me realize that my story could inspire others who were also faced with adversity. That pushed me to finish the book that Andréa and I had begun together. She wanted to let people know that anything can be overcome with determination. Completing the book and receiving the gift of Jane's foreword also gave me the confidence to offer women's retreats called "Inspiring Women, Inspiring Stories," because I believe that we can all grow and learn from each other's journeys through adversity.

After talking with so many people who have gone through a tragedy or seemingly insurmountable challenge, I would say that if you find yourself falling and stumbling backwards into the depths of devastation, you may thrust forward and find yourself going beyond what you'd ever expect yourself capable of if you are lucky enough to be surrounded by incredibly supportive people, are receptive to this support, and embrace the positive energy that is offered. (To this day, fifteen years after my daughter's death, her friends send me flowers for Mother's Day with the cards signed, "From your girls.") I think that there was something inside of me that wanted to go toward the light, rather than darkness. I grasped at any light that gave me comfort and some hope.

Hope is a tricky word. I think that the hope that other parents perceive in my work is that you can go on and maintain closeness with your loved one, however spiritual you are. I believe I will see my daughter again, and I believe that she is looking down from above and has her hand in the miraculous things that have made this foundation successful.

If I have one message to people going through difficult times, it is this: remain open to all the love and help that people offer (whether it's just taking a quiet walk with you or a dinner invitation or just being there to listen). Reach back with gratitude and let them know their gestures of kindness and thoughtfulness are helpful and appreciated. This creates an ongoing healing cycle of giving and receiving that will carry you through the difficult times.

—**Susan Rizzo Vincent**, author of *Dréa's Dream: An Unfinished Dance—Lessons in Love, Loss, Hope and Healing*

Open to Possibilities, Not Limitations

In a hospital's pediatric ward, you either feel blessed because it's not your child or cursed because it is. My daughter had her first seizure at nine months old and was diagnosed with epilepsy three months later. I've spent a lot of time in pediatrics feeling cursed.

In January 2014, a friend asked me to paddle to Catalina, run the Catalina Marathon, and then paddle home. I decided I would do it for my daughter. I couldn't stop Callie's seizures, but I could dedicate my race to her. Thus, Callie's Cause was born and sixty of us paddled to Catalina. We also held the first annual Callie's Cause Auction at Duke's. In the end, we raised $56,000 for UCLA's Pediatric Neurology Department.

The most important outcome of Callie's Cause was the change in me. The moment I decided to paddle for Callie, I opened my heart to the possibilities of Callie's diagnosis instead of dwelling on its limitations. As we again paddle to Catalina, my hope is that Callie's Cause will be the blessing for others that it has been for me.

—Darlene Addison

The Baby Ring

Many years ago, my daughter Leah died in a tragic accident at nine months old. I left her in front of the house with my husband. Unfortunately, he ran over her in the driveway. I came out a minute later and found her, already dead. It was the most devastating thing of my life! My precious baby was gone and I was no longer a mother.

Right before we closed her casket, I thought, "Oh, her baby ring, I want that with me."

I gently took the ring off her finger. I had on a dress with no pockets, so I stuck it on the end of my pinky finger to take it home, and I never took it off. Fortunately, I got pregnant again twice. The marriage was abusive so the three of us escaped with a trash bag of toys and bag of clothes. We made it back across the country to my parents' home where they took us in and filled us with love, safety, and peace.

Several years later I remarried a man who was a widower with four small children. One child was taken but I was given a bounty. Together we raised the six children, and it was a beautiful blessing in my life. Eighteen years later, after the children were grown and launched into the world, I discovered my husband had fallen in love with another woman. I was blindsided! I hit the floor and curled up in the fetal position for about six months.

One evening I had an AHA moment when I thought, "Wait a minute, I don't have to stay here. The kids are grown and gone, and I can't heal in this town."

That led me to put everything I owned in storage, and travel in developing countries by myself for a year. I volunteered in Tanzania, Africa, for three months and it was amazing.

While there, one morning I went out for a run and as I passed through a village a teenage girl came running out of her shack screaming, "Help me! Help me!"

I went in with her and we discovered her sister was holding a dead baby in her arms. All of the feelings of baby Leah came rushing back into my body full force. I helped these young women for about four hours, and when I left them I ran straight behind a patch of trees, hurled my guts out, and sobbed. I had no idea that much grief was still buried after twenty-eight years.

I began to realize the grief was still there because I didn't talk about Leah very much through the years. The conversation just doesn't come up; even people who did know I lost a baby, didn't know how to talk to me about it either. I began to wonder how many other people are grieving silently over the loss of a child, unable to process the grief long-term and have support. I looked down at my pinky finger to the beloved baby ring still there, and an AHA hit me again.

I want to help open up the conversation and make it easier to talk about a child's death. It's like cancer was back in the seventies. No one ever spoke the "C" word, until someone brilliantly came up with the Pink Ribbon. Now speaking of cancer is less taboo and people can grieve the tragedy openly and have support.

So I started The Baby Ring Movement. When someone has lost a child, he or she goes to a jewelry store, gets a baby ring, and puts it on the pinky finger.

When others see the ring they can ask, "Oh you lost a child? Tell me about your beloved."

This movement also includes miscarriage, for that is just as devastating and even more of a secret. My dream is that the Baby Ring will open the conversation with the same power as the Pink Ribbon, and parents can process the grief with support. I also hope that parents will find each other and form a bond. Let's help everyone move through the devastation.

You can read Leah's story in my memoir, *It's Already Tomorrow Here.*

—**Lucetta Zaytoun**

Building a Support System for Caregivers

I divorced my only daughter's father when she was a year old. Dan and I had met in college. He was tall, blond, mischievous, and funny. When he asked me to marry him, I remember thinking "What if no one else ever asked me?" and so I said "Yes."

We'd been together more than three years when I finally piled the boxes by the front door and told Dan it was over. Drinking had been his favorite pastime since the day we met, but it was college and everyone drank. He promised to quit for years but every night he would linger at the bar before coming home. Then, one evening in a drunken stupor, he backhanded me. I refused to be the abused wife and I certainly would not allow my precious child to be exposed to this torture, so at age twenty-four, I found myself divorced with a one-year-old. I worked fulltime to survive, while my mother, then retired, cared for my daughter. I remember standing in front of the mirror. I gave myself a pep talk, "A tiny being is depending on you, so get out there and find a better job."

I was the only child of wonderful parents who had anxiously awaited my arrival for more than ten years. It was a simple but perfect childhood filled with love. Mom always instilled a sense of gratitude and a "glass half full" attitude within me. As I approached my high school graduation, I realized that both of my parents had come from simple beginnings and struggled, so budgeting for my higher education was not in their plan. I took a fulltime job and put myself through junior college.

As with so many women raising their children alone, you do whatever is necessary to provide for your children. As a divorced mom, receiving no support from my ex, I worked two and three jobs to provide for my daughter, making sure she had the opportunities of private school and college.

My daughter was ten and I was still a single mom when I took on what would be one of the biggest challenges of my life. I became the guardian of my best friend's 15-year-old daughter. Laura was only eight when her mother, my friend, died tragically in a car accident. Now her grandma, who'd been her guardian, no longer wanted to deal with a teenager. Laura had dropped out of school and was spiraling. We had to find a way to help this girl or we might lose her. My daughter was thrilled with the idea of a "big sister," and I promptly took on a second daughter along with her 100-pound husky, her cat, fish, bird, and all her mom's possessions. Through three and a half years of daily calls from the school counselor, endless caring for the menagerie, and seven fender benders, Laura managed to graduate from high school. Now forty-three, Laura just completed her bachelor's degree and is going for her master's. My biological daughter, Tracie, also made it through those chaotic years. Now thirty-seven, she is a successful business-woman, just completed her MBA, and is an incredible mom to my two perfect granddaughters.

My folks lived a quiet life in retirement, remaining in my childhood home with their two little dogs. Every Saturday, I would stop by to do my mother's hair. This ritual would span nearly thirty years. The aroma of one of mom's famous desserts would swirl through my nostrils as I entered the house. With "curling" complete, Mom, Dad, and I would enjoy coffee and sweets, and catch up on the week's events.

Dad was a good man but due to a hearing loss as a teen, he was always a bit of a yeller. He was slightly shy but compensated with a great sense of humor. He and mom had been married nearly fifty-five years when I realized something was different. He was always a screamer but now he would start an argument—but then not recall why he was angry.

My folks enjoyed outings with their church seniors group. One day, I received a frantic call from the group coordinator, saying they were at the zoo and had lost my father. Dad had simply wandered off. I immediately drove to the zoo and when I arrived, the coordinator, with the entire senior group in tow, had located my father on the other side of the park. This adventure and a visit to the doctor, confirmed my suspicions. Dad had Alzheimer's.

Thus, began my twelve-year journey of caregiving for Dad, Mom, and dear uncle Earl. My life felt like a three-ring circus, performing nothing short of a juggling act. I worked fulltime while fulfilling my roles as wife, mother, and grandmother, all the while managing the care, health, finances, and safety of three elderly people. I learned every conceivable aspect of caring for elders: Medicare versus Medicaid; wills and trusts; powers of attorney (POAs); assisted living and fire safety; long-distance care and Veterans' Benefits; do-not-resuscitate orders (DNRs) and living wills; nursing homes and adult daycares; oxygen and medications; food service and feeding; Depends; clinical depression and congestive heart failure; and crematoriums and funeral homes.

After twelve years of caregiving and another four years working through the health issues precipitated by the stress of caregiving, I finally came out of the fog. Most people might have pulled their life back together and never looked back. However, because of my own personal experiences, I felt compelled to help other nonpaid family caregivers. I leveraged my personal expertise and knowledge to create CarolCARE—a firm dedicated to offering support, empowerment, and hope to caregivers, not only live through the perils of caregiving but also to find quality of life after caregiving.

Currently, there are more than 65 million nonpaid family caregivers in the US, and with 10,000 Boomers turning sixty-five every day for the next thirteen years, we are facing a seismic event. Caring for an elderly family member is a daunting task, no matter what level of care is needed. Until you've have lived in the trenches of family caregiving, you cannot possibly understand the staggering effect it will have on every aspect of your life: health, finances, mental well-being; jobs; and other relationships.

No matter what challenge you face, look for the positive and find a way to keep moving forward. Honestly, I am so incredibly grateful every day for everything and everyone in my life. I never take myself too seriously and have a good sense of humor. With the loss of many friends in recent years, I remind myself that life goes by so incredibly quickly, so I can't waste a minute of it. Did you know that if you live to be eighty, that is only 960 months of life? Seriously! Stop whining, stop playing games on your phone, and live every minute of every single day to its fullest. Every day is a chance for a new adventure. Who knows where you might go and whom you may meet?

Finally, I'm sending a hug your way and remember to "always take good care of yourself first."

—**Carol Core**, author of
50 Sanity Saving Tips for Caregivers

More Than a Place to Stay—A Community

"Live each day as if it were your last." We are all familiar with this quote. In my past life, the life where everything was still right, I never quite knew what to make of this quote. At that time, I would think about what I would do if I knew today was my last day alive. I certainly wouldn't go to work. That's an easy one, but that's where reality and the quote don't quite jive. Obviously you can't live each day like it is your last or you would never go to work. So I would tell myself that this is a nice idea but not exactly a workable concept.

When Doug was diagnosed, it didn't take a genius to see just how serious the situation was. My searches on the internet only made things worse. It was very obvious that the odds were not with us growing old together. I could no longer wake up each day and pretend that there were many more days left in our life together. I couldn't hug him and not wonder how many of these hugs were left. This is when I realized that whoever first said, "Live each day like it is your last." had it wrong. The quote should be, "Live each day like it is the last of everyone you encounter." I wonder what the world would be like if we all did this.

What I remember most about the first few days following 9/11 was how kind everyone was to each other. People didn't honk impatiently at other drivers while commuting to and from work. We seemed to look at each other as common victims in a horrible tragedy. Somehow compassion was our first response. Although a personal tragedy or obstacle may not be as immense as 9/11, I know that almost everyone I encounter who knows about Doug's death and my own battle with cancer has been very kind to me.

What I also know is that everyone has a story. Everyone who isn't in the midst of some personal struggle has overcome some tragedy or difficulty. It would be wonderful if we didn't need to know about someone's loss or have some outward sign, like baldness, to prompt compassion and kindness each day.

The concept of Open Doors came to me when I was caring for my husband. When I stayed with him in the hospital, I talked to many people in the waiting area or in the halls. We shared our stories and I found that so many people wanted to be with their loved ones but had no money to travel or a hotel to stay at while their loved one was being treated.

After a nurse asked me to try to comfort a widow whose husband had passed away after four years of struggling with an illness, I realized that I had a window of opportunity. So many family and friends wanted to help me out and contribute in some way. I didn't need financial help but I knew that plenty of people did. I began to think about starting a place—a house—where people could talk and help each other.

The nurses and doctors were so compassionate with me and I wanted to give that back. We found a beautiful Victorian house in downtown Indianapolis near the hospital and opened it for families of patients waiting for a bone marrow transplant at Indiana University Hospital.

The Good House is essentially a bed & breakfast. Guests receive a welcome basket with some treats and a handwritten note, and there are cheerful decorations around the house made by local elementary school kids. Sometimes there are four guests, sometimes eight at a time. And the house is completely managed by a rotating group of volunteers who will come in clean, cook, and maintain the house. We raise money at fundraisers and through donations. At some point, I may need a larger house, but I don't want it to lose the feel that The Good House has.

The hospital's social workers and bone marrow coordinators know about the Good House and identify patients who have a need. It's the most rewarding thing I have ever done. People don't talk about the money they are saving but how grateful they are for the community and the love that they feel as soon as they walk into the door. You see the beauty and the humanity in the guests and the volunteers.

—**Becky Armbruster**, thegoodhouse.org

The Impossible

I was thirty-seven years old, overweight, on extra-strength antidepressants, and could barely run around the block. I was a young single mom and had battled some very dark moments. Looking in the mirror disgusted me—until I began running. Running saved my life, and now I'm using it to help save the lives of other people.

I first began running on the beach, just hoping to run continuously from one lifeguard tower to the next. Even that small goal seemed impossible, but with my dog Jessie alongside me, I kept going. Even at the snail's pace I was keeping then, I immediately felt more healthy and positive. I had caught the running bug. Right away, my dad became my biggest fan and for the first time in my life, I felt he was truly proud of me. As I was getting myself into much better physical and emotional shape, I faced another enormous challenge. My father, age seventy-five, was diagnosed with pancreatic cancer. When he passed away from the disease, just thirty-five days after his diagnosis, I knew I had to do something *BIG* in his honor. I had to find a way to fight this awful disease. I decided I would run fifty-two marathons in fifty-two weeks. I wasn't sure how I would do it, but I was determined to reach that goal, on behalf of my father who had always supported me.

I hoped that I would raise a lot of money in honor of my father and to help other people. But I never expected to be featured in the inspiring documentary *Spirit of the Marathon II*. Nor could I have anticipated all the media attention I would receive. I didn't expect that my ambitious but deeply personal fifty-two marathons in fifty-two weeks goal would become a movement.

I continue to run and fundraise to find a cure for pancreatic cancer. I also hope that I can inspire people to take on causes or issues that are important to them. You can do anything you want. While this idea may seem impossible now, because you have not yet done it, take it from me—I had never done anything like this before. But once you do something extraordinary, then you will realize that you can do anything. Your objective may require some planning or adjustments as you work toward whatever you want to achieve. First, figure out what "it" you want to do, create a plan and then get started!

And once you do one "it" successfully, then the doors will open and other amazing "its" will come your way.

—**Julie Weiss**, marathongoddess.com

A Bionic Teacher Passionate About STEM

I know about rockets and robot camps. Seriously, my passion is STEM and inspiring young people to learn about science and technology, and empowering them to develop their innate skills and talents. I'm in the midst of writing several books targeted at different age groups on this topic.

When I'm asked to describe myself, I say that I'm a bionic renaissance woman, a curriculum advisor, writer, and very active in working with "at risk" kids and empowering them to develop their potential and their future success. (In the past, I was much more involved in helping the homeless, but these days I work more with kids and STEM.) But most of all, I'm an engaged person in life.

At age nineteen, I was diagnosed with rheumatoid arthritis, which really knocked me for a loop. Since then, I've had forty surgeries and have artificial knees, a hip, and shoulders. I have faced numerous health challenges including two minor strokes. Through all of these health challenges, I stay very positive, grateful for what *does* work and focus on making an impact, locally and nationally.

My attitude of gratitude comes from my early family life. I was one of seven siblings and our lives were dysfunctional. Somehow, I always had a positive and grateful perspective.

And going through my health issues, I thought, "I've been knocked down and now I have to come right back up."

I always try to see where the blessing is in any situation. When I counsel kids who have endured horrible situations, I listen until they can't talk anymore. Then, I help them start their lives anew from that point.

We don't understand how powerful we all are. Innately, as human beings, we are all for one, and one for all. Everyone can be of service to other people, even in the most minuscule way. We must support each other in order to be the best we can be. You can't give a blessing without receiving a blessing in return.

When we interact on a one-on-one basis, we can recognize other people's talents and strengths even when they don't recognize these traits themselves. We are all good people but we just forget that. We as human beings have opportunities to bless people and change their situations.

—Nola Garcia de Quevedo, author of *Golden Ideas to Inspire You*; CEO and Director of StarBot

In Honor of Young Heroes

Life works in mysterious and sometimes heartbreaking ways. But when we come out on the other side, we are often different people, with new goals, new priorities, and new outlooks on life.

Our lives changed forever on October 21, 2010. My son, three weeks after his twenty-second birthday, was diagnosed with an inoperable malignant brain tumor. Everybody always says how amazing I am for leaving my job to be with him 24/7 and working with him and his fantabulous medical team nonstop to ensure he made it through. But he's the amazing one—my hero, my survivor—leading a different life than we ever imagined, but thriving in his own right, always on the road to self-sufficiency. And I consider us so very lucky. My child is a survivor. We have met many families who have not been so lucky. Our good friend, Joanne Mayo, whom we met through the pediatric brain tumor community, lost her daughter— Cailin. She's the one I admire every day. I'm not the amazing mama; she is. Her daughter lives in her heart, in every beautiful moon, whenever she sees a Disney character, a hedgehog, or even a baby giraffe. That's bravery, facing each day when her oldest child will be forever nineteen. My son calls Joanne his Michigan Mama, and she's always there for us.

But on this other side, I learned so much, about survival instincts, about the brain, about people, about way too many other families in the pediatric brain tumor and pediatric cancer communities. And I learned about giving back and how important that is. Some of our closest friends come from these communities because they know, they understand, they get it. Your child is not just cured of cancer or a brain tumor and voila, the world goes back to normal. There is no normal— just a new normal every day.

On our journey, we found amazing help and resources from two organizations in particular. The Michael Magro Foundation (michaelmagrofoundation.com), which helps families here on Long Island (NY) where a child's been diagnosed with cancer, gives tens of thousands of dollars every year to the Cancer

Center for Kids where my son was treated. Paul and Terrie Magro, who have become good friends, started the foundation in memory of their son Michael. Again, they are the amazing ones, moving on by honoring their son's memory every day and paying it forward anyway they can. And the Children's Brain Tumor Foundation (cbtf.org) provides wonderful resources and support including a Young Adult Survivors Group.

While my son was in the hospital I knew I could never go back to my previous place of employment—I was not leaving him to caretakers—I was going to do it my way with 24/7 encouragement and lots of prayers. So I left the firm I was with for twenty years and started my own public relations agency. Running my own business gives me the latitude to devote a portion of time to these two organizations handling a wide range of publicity activities for both organizations from arranging event listings, media coverage, media interviews, MCs for events, soliciting gift donations, coordinating events, and so forth.

My message to others is to never give up hope and always look to the future, whether it's the future you imagined or one that has been dropped in your lap by a traumatic turn of events. And one last thing—be kind. You never know what someone else has dealt with or is dealing with. In this age of transparency, many things are still invisible.

—**Lori Ames**, mother of a hero and founder
of ThePRFreelancer, Inc.

Part Seven

Self-Exploration and Survival

Your journey through life will change whether or not you expect it. Sometimes, you've planned everything from marriage to buying a house to having children to getting that promotion at work. Then something happens and you have to change direction. It can be difficult and the decisions you make may cause a rift between your friends and your family. Ultimately, you make the choices that determine the direction of your life. Sometimes, all you can do is take one baby step to get out bed but doing that is helping create a new path. Trust me, I've experienced more than my fair share of these devastating and frightening changes. Because of this so many people have asked me if I'm some kind of Phoenix rising from the ashes! I explain that my mother's mantra "that there is always someone worse off than you" is so true, and having a purpose in life is the key to surviving and thriving with change.

When You Are Falling, Dive Instead

How did I go from dining at the luxurious and decadent "Vertigo" rooftop bar in Bangkok to my fate being decided in a dilapidated 1940s townhouse in an unsavory neighborhood in Frankfurt, Germany? The continuous tape in my head repeated like a mantra, "This is not really happening." But it was. The insultingly sunny day found me with only $158 to my name climbing the stairs of that run-down house, with its peeling paint and worn red carpet, to a private detective's office. How had this happened? In a blink of an eye I had gone from a life I loved—I had a beautiful, loving family, a husband who was my best friend, an elegant home that we had built, and was living a privileged life abroad—to standing across from Herr Schmidt sitting behind his pompous oak desk, feeling lost in the enormous room with thick cigar smoke choking the air. It felt surreal. It all started three weeks earlier. While driving home from an afternoon event at my children's school in the Taunus Mountains of central Germany, I had received a text message. I waited for a red light to read it. The text informed me that all of my credit cards had been canceled, that my debit card would no longer work; and that, if I needed money, I could borrow $100 until I could pay it back. The last line read, "I hope you have a pleasant afternoon anyway." My husband had abandoned us.

I'd never had a panic attack before. I had always dismissed them as self-induced drama created when someone was unable to deal with her life. Well, life was about to set me straight on that point. I panicked. Hands shaking and with a strangled voice, I called a friend and asked her to meet me at home. I hoped I would get there in one piece.

There was nothing to be done. All financial doors were closed. Apparently, I hadn't been listed as co-owner of the accounts my husband and I had set up when I first moved to Germany twenty-five years earlier and didn't speak the language. I could not access any of our accounts anymore and I noticed that all of our financial records were no longer on the top shelf in our study. I still owned half of the house, but I had given up my career, had two children to care for, and my parents lived an ocean away with challenges of their own. It had been hard enough for me lately.

My father, who lived in Colorado, had been going through heart failure. I had been visiting frequently to help care for him and to get his "things in order." I knew what was coming soon enough, but I didn't want to go there in my mind. But it was no use; the thought of losing him consumed me. The ten-hour flights weren't easy, to say the least, with my head full and my heart heavy.

At the same time, and despite her naturally cheerful spirit that had earned her the title of family ambassador, my beautiful 13-year-old daughter had fallen into a deep depression when our family began to crumble.

"I'm having dark thoughts, Mama," she told me one morning as she buttered her toast in our sunny breakfast nook.

"What kind of dark thoughts?" I asked, fearing the worst.

"Well, I'm too chicken to hurt myself—I think—but I don't want to be alive anymore."

Dark couldn't nearly begin to name what I felt hearing those words. I felt like I was beginning to fall, sliding slowly down a bottomless black hole.

One thing I'm good at is taking action when necessary. So, I shifted into crisis mode. I had been doing that a lot lately, this time for my sweet child. I called for an emergency appointment with the pediatrician who set up daily therapy sessions, keeping her at home with me rather than a clinic, to the great relief of my own breaking heart. The school was informed, counselors updated, and friends jumped in to support me as I supported my child. "This is not really happening," I kept thinking.

While all of this was going on, my son was finishing his last year of high school and ramping up the college application process. We worked as a team through the myriad of documents with the goal for him to go to a good school in the U.S., but that would mean he would be leaving home, far from home. It was a natural and good change, for him, but another factor that pushed me farther down the slippery sides of that deep cavern of despair.

By this time, I was devastated by the ground beneath me cracking and leaving such a gaping hole. I couldn't sleep, became intimate with panic attacks, and had lost forty-nine pounds in three months. I had to ask friends to remind me of the simplest of things, like doctor's appointments, picking up the children, and going grocery shopping. Overnight, it seemed, my life went from a star-studded success to a show-stopping mess. My heart was shattered, and I felt helpless.

Worst of all, was my loss of belief in any goodness in the world and my loss of faith in God. I agonized over the erosion of my spiritual foundation that was no longer recognizable. All the tools I'd worked for so hard—that had helped me heal and thrive after a violent and lonely childhood, that had helped me finally become a happy, confident, nonjudgmental person—felt unavailable to me. Tears, fear, and anger ruled me way too often now. What had happened to *me*? How unfair was life? How cruel must God be that I was back at this place of pain and suffering again after so much personal transformation?

Amidst this chaos, my dear friend came to help me sort and organize my office. Me, the business major! I was unable to do basic filing. So, Lotten came to my rescue. She spread all our files, *sans* financials, across our large wooden dining table and dug in.

Midway she called me over. "Check this out. It looks like these are bank statements. Did you know you had these accounts?"

I was gobsmacked. In my state of pain, I had swallowed the story that there was no money left in savings due to my carelessness with our resources. With that belief, I'd also swallowed a whole lot of guilt. But here were statements from three banks where we had accounts for twenty-five years, accounts I had no recollection of until I saw the statements. Stress, I was learning, was a formidable force. Unfortunately, my name wasn't listed on any of them.

I needed to be able to prove to a court that the accounts were active, perhaps with money still in them. So I went in search of help, and I found a private detective. I had to borrow money to pay his steep fee, but I made the appointment and set off for his office. Entering the smoky room, I saw only one other piece of furniture beside his desk, a worn black swivel chair facing Herr Schmidt. I sank into it slowly, gripping my white envelope stuffed with borrowed cash.

He told me, "I don't make promises, you'll get no receipt, and there's no refund, whether I find something out or not."

"If the accounts do still exist will you write a report on your letterhead and sign it?" I asked. Yes, that was possible. It was something at least.

As I walked back down those rickety stairs, I had an epiphany. Maybe it was the descent from that smoky room in that broken house back toward the sunshine. Maybe it was the culmination of so much heartache and degradation. Or, maybe it was the hand of God gently pushing me down to the ground of my being until I was spread so thin that there was nowhere else to go but to surrender.

In that moment, I suddenly realized that if I am falling, I may as well dive. Give in. Give it up. Let go, totally. Dive with purpose as deep as I needed in order to dwell full time in my heart, not allowing my core to be shattered, or even shaken, by events that take place outside of me.

My father used to tell me, "No one, Leeza, no one is bigger than God." I got it Dad. When I dove into what I was intensely resisting I could finally feel God's presence.

I began reflecting on recent events. I had been able to secure my daughter's safety and her heart was slowly mending. My son had been accepted to UCLA and was on his way to launching into a bright future. My father had loved his life, and I had sat beside him when he left this world, completely at peace with ending a life well lived. But why was I still shaking my fist and stomping my foot at what I'd been dealt? Why did I still believe that I was at the mercy of the people and events in my life?

In that moment, on those tattered stairs in that dingy brown house now an ocean away, I realized that there were two possibilities to explain everything. One possibility was that my beliefs—the God I had found, the belief that I'd held strongly that goodness exists in every person, and love always prevails—were empty promises, self-created fantasies to help us get through life.

The other possibility literally took my breath away as I finally let go to free fall into that eternal space. Was it possible that the God I had found was, indeed, amazingly creative in choreographing all of this? That my prayers for harmony and joy and peace were actually being answered through circumstances that looked chaotic, that I could not yet understand? That goodness absolutely lives in everyone, yet some people forget that it's there, and when they do they can do some horrendous things to themselves and to others?

Was it possible in the very circumstances I had so resisted—the crumbling of our family and life that I so dearly loved—more goodness than I could imagine was actually taking place? Perhaps I was simply unable to see that new birth occurring because I was too deeply involved in witnessing the destruction. Was it possible, as this second option suggests, that an even more beautiful life than I could have imagined was in the offing, and that the highest good for each of us was being brought forth under circumstances that had the appearance of being hurtful and destructive?

And, if all that *were* possible, didn't that then mean that my happiness and well-being rely solely on which lens I choose when looking at all of the events that had taken place? The loss of money and our home, the restructuring of our family, the passing of my father, my daughter's pain, and my son's departure could all be seen as blessings instead of burdens. Was that possible? Yes, I have found, yes it is.

What I now know is that the perspective we decide to have is the deciding factor in our life. It is not what we are looking at, but what we are looking from that determines how we experience what life throws at us. The cause of our joy and of our pain is within us. How liberating is that? We are the masters of our own world. That possibility places us squarely in the driver's seat of our own lives.

After that realization, I found the power to move the three of us to the U.S, establish a new home, and start again. I opened my own coaching and consulting business, wrote another book, and I have built a new life. Most important, I love myself and those around me. I am that happy, confident, loving person again. I chose to look through the lens that showed it was all for the highest and best. Yes, indeed, when you are falling, dive instead!

—**Leeza Carlone Steindorf**, author of *Connected Parent,*
Empowered Child: Five Keys to Raising Happy,
Confident, Responsible Kids

Learning a New Language
by Listening to the Radio

I wanted a different life from what I had in Russia. Staying there meant I couldn't travel and see the world. I always dreamt of being in New York.

I came to the United States when I was twenty-six years old. I did have one uncle here with whom I lived for a few months, but I had no friends and didn't know the English language. I was given some financial assistance from the American Association for New Americans. From the day I arrived, I absolutely knew I was in the right place.

I wanted to be in the entertainment business but there was no way for me to function in that field when I first arrived because I couldn't understand the language or express myself. It was especially hard for someone like me, who used language at a sophisticated level to write and perform in Russia where I had done stand-up comedy.

In a funny way, my decisions to leave Russia helped prepare me to find work here. While waiting for my visa, I was seen as a traitor and couldn't get a full-time job. In order to support myself in my homeland, I learned to be a masseuse and also how to do illustrations.

In New York, I rented a space and got massage clients. In between massages, I worked on my portfolio so I could get illustration jobs. I listened to public radio for hours as a way to learn English. Listening allowed me to become fluent enough to get back to writing and performing. When I first came, I thought I would cut off my entire Russian background, and I was absorbed with becoming an American and a New Yorker. But my attitude changed and my stand-up character was, in fact, me, someone with exposure both to Russian and American cultures. Both cultures are incredibly rich and I ended up using both of them in my work.

I came here as an adult, having endured hardships in Russia. I had no problems with what other people might consider difficult such as a long commute or some of the hassles that come with life in New York. I didn't expect things to come easy so I had no disappointments or hard times.

Life has been much richer here so I know emigrating was the right decision for me. It might be a cliché but I could do whatever I wanted without limitations. I wanted to get ahead and learn and I knew that in time I would make money. Once I became comfortable with my English, I went back to doing comedy, which I loved, and it led to a deal with HBO.

In Russia, you had limited opportunities and you couldn't be an entrepreneur. Your work options were always pre-set. Here, I am embracing completely a life that I have chosen. Every day I'm doing what I want to do.

If you were born here and have support systems of friends and families, it may seem that it would be hard to start a new life at age twenty-six. But I don't view my path as unique. If you believe in yourself and what you can do, then go ahead and pursue your dreams. Don't settle for a different path. Don't be sad. Keep moving ahead. It's impossible not to reach your goals in this society and environment. I feel that, especially in New York, there is support around every corner. There is someone or something that will help you advance your goals.

For anyone facing any challenge, I would say, Just Go and Do It!

—**Sasha Vosk**, author of *A Pictorial History of New York: A Comparative View from 1600s to the Present*

The Road to Freedom

Sitting here on the secluded patio, I am mesmerized as the afternoon shadows stretch and the golden tones dance on the pavement. Suddenly I am transported to my first bridal show.

It was April 1985 and the city was magical. It was filled with tall glass buildings, Cadillacs and Rolls Royces, men in cowboy hats and boots, and women with their big hair, gloves, and hats all very glamourous.

Dallas was my dream place to live in. It was the TV series *Dallas* that was my escape all those Friday nights. The show transported me into a world of make-believe, a world that I yearned to be in. Everything I learned about fashion was from watching the women on the show.

Before leaving Bangkok to present my designs for the first time at a bridal show, my family asked me, "Why are you wasting time and money going to a foreign land for yet another failure in your life?" I just smiled and thought to myself, they will never get me, will they?

I was born in Bangkok, Thailand, into an Indian Sikh family, into the sect that in those days was extremely strict, orthodox, and conservative. My first recollection is wondering if I had been switched at birth because I looked so unlike my five siblings.

My skin was the wrong color and consequently, I was unwanted.

To compensate for the lack of attention at home I rebelled at every chance just to be seen and heard. I believe my parents did not know what to do with me. So at the age of nine I was sent to a Catholic convent boarding school in India, which became my home. I excelled at the school and went on to attend college in New Delhi.

Arranged marriages were the norm, and when I refused to agree to one, I was denied further studies and locked up for months until I realized that I had no choice but to comply. Forced into a marriage at age eighteen to a man who had nothing to his name, I had to become the breadwinner to support the seven family members living in our tiny home, along with three children who soon arrived.

I felt lost and alone, especially since my husband became a religious fanatic and abused me every chance he got, parading me with my eyes black and blue and my nose broken in front of his guru and congregation just to show me who was the boss, and to show everyone how macho he was.

I opened a tailoring shop at a prestigious hotel in Bangkok to make ends meet. It was there that I received the break of a lifetime, one that I believed would get me out of the hell I found myself in. I wanted so desperately to give my children a better life, far away from the oppression and abuse, and removed from the controlling guru and the culture that was enveloping them as well.

My client from San Antonio invited me to bring my ready-to-wear collection to help her with a charity event she was hosting. I agreed, much to the dismay and disapproval of my husband and his family.

The show was a huge success but little did I know that it would be the finale piece of the show, the only wedding dress I had ever designed, that would change my life forever. I was invited to show my "Bridal Collection" in Dallas.

On April 15, 1985, I was showing my first ever bridal collection at the Dallas Apparel Mart. The first two days were disheartening. I saw no orders, and buyers would walk by my showroom gasping at what they saw.

At a time when the American bride wore only white, all sixteen pieces of my wedding collection were in color. I had not done my homework thinking that since Asian brides only wore color that the entire world did so too. I was devastated at the lack of business, having spent all my money on my collection and on travel. Perhaps my family was right. Perhaps I really was a failure...

The Universe had other plans though. I walked into the building on the third morning and saw my face staring back at me from the front page of the *Dallas Apparel News* and could not believe what I saw. The headline read: "St. Pucchi Designs Dream-Like Gowns." I was hailed as a pioneer for introducing color and pure silk to the American bridal scene. The bridal world as we knew it would change forever. Orders started pouring in, and I knew the Universe had my back.

Soon I was able to convince my husband that we should move to Dallas to grow the business. My children were happy and I prayed that my husband would change and be kinder, and find peace in our new home. Away from the guru and his family he would not feel so pressured to prove his masculinity, and we could be a loving family unit that I so longed to experience.

However, no matter how hard I tried, things got from bad to worse. Ever so controlling, my husband became more obsessed with wanting to keep me away from interacting and even speaking to any of my clients. If my staff asked me questions he would push me aside and answer. His word was law. At home, he would not lift a finger to help and told the children that they should not either. All of a sudden, I was the only one keeping the house and family fed and clothed, and my business running by day, while spending my nights designing and communicating with my factory in Thailand to make sure orders were being produced in a timely manner. Not only that but the physical and emotional abuse became worse as days and months and years went by.

I finally reached the conclusion that there was no hope, especially because my children were witnessing the horrible abuse every day. I knew it was wrong for them to think that it was acceptable for a man to treat his wife this way.

Having no access to finances since he controlled everything I did not think I had any way out. However, one day the beatings grew so intense that I thought he would surely kill me. I knew I had to get away to keep my sanity and protect my children. I was able to sneak away to consult a divorce lawyer. My attorney came to the conclusion that the only solution was for me to run away and remain in hiding until the court hearing. I decided at least to take my two younger children with me, but I was told that I would then be charged with kidnapping, which would make the case more difficult to resolve in my favor.

Six months seemed like eternity. I was in hiding and could not see my babies. Finally, the ordeal was over and the court granted me custody of my children. On the day I was to reunite with them, I found the house empty, my children gone, and my business in bankruptcy. My husband had taken the children to Thailand, essentially kidnapping them. Everything that mattered to me had been taken away from me.

I fought for custody in Thailand for eight years. Having lived in Asia and faced the legal system in Asia I knew all too well how oppressed women were there. I begged my family to help me but no one wanted any part of it. In their eyes, I had brought shame to my family and to be associated with me was not in their best interest.

My spirit was broken, but I knew I had to move on. I had to revive my company, to earn enough money and make sure that my children, although no longer in my life, were taken care of. I wanted them to have all the comforts that I could provide along with a good education. Everything I did was for them.

When all was lost, my business became my baby. I poured my heart and soul into it. I did become a favorite of celebrities and the media and a famous designer. And I won several nominations and awards as Best Bridal Designer. To everyone looking at me it was apparent that I had it all. Inside, however, my heart was crying...

When all seemed lost I turned within and sought strength through prayer and meditation. In my spare moments, I read books by spiritual and inspirational masters: Dr. Wayne Dyer, Thich Nhat Hanh, Eckhart Tolle, Byron Katie, and Osho, among others. I was inspired most of all by the late Sufi poet Rumi, even designing entire bridal collections around his poems. I grasped at every word I could that would seep into my soul and give me peace and acceptance of my life, such as it was.

And most of all I worked on forgiveness. Not for anyone, but for my own inner peace. The rewards of inner peace, happiness, and knowing my true essence were well worth the emotional pain.

My heart is heavy but my conscience is clear. I did everything I could to protect and help my children and even though we do not have a life together, I know that I did what was important for me.

Nobody said that healing past wounds would be easy. It takes courage to bring to the surface and accept the things that have caused suffering, especially things that you cannot change.

It takes a level of self-love, of dedication, and determination to rise above all that is blocking you from living your greatest life. Look at every area of your life and ask yourself: How is this serving me? Is this helping me grow mentally, emotionally, and spiritually? Does being in this place and holding on to anger, hurt, and blame bring me peace? Make the tough but necessary decision to let go of anything that is blocking that and preventing you from living your greatest life.

"The wound is the place where the Light enters you." ~Rumi

—**Rani St. Pucchi**, ranistpucchi.com/author of several
books including *The Soulmate Checklist:
Keys to Finding Your Perfect Partner*

Fostering a Dog Gave Me Purpose

My wife Johanna and I had been married about seven years. We had bought a house but never really discussed having children. When we decided not to become parents, I was upset. I began talking about getting a dog. I had dogs when I was growing up though Joanna did not.

We decided that we would foster a rescue dog from an organization we knew about. We were vetted, almost as if we were fostering a child. There was a home visit and we needed a plan for where the dog would be while we worked. Sydney came into our home and within weeks, we knew we wanted to keep her.

We weren't home from 7 a.m. to 5 p.m. weekdays but that meant our weekends and the rest of our time would be focused around Sydney. That was ideal; Sydney filled the void that we both felt, but never discussed.

Then I lost my job and was home for about a year. I had no prospects for work and my severance was running out. I was home all day and Johanna suggested that we foster another dog so that I would have something other than "not having a job" to focus on during the day.

We got Ruby, the world's sweetest dog. She loved to walk, which allowed me to discover my neighborhood. Since I had no routine because I wasn't working, she forced me to create one. I took her for a walk, then spent time job-searching, and later played with her. It gave me a sense of normalcy and a purpose amidst searching for a job when you don't feel you're wanted or needed. Ruby wanted and needed me.

I was doing something instead of brooding and being unemployed. Ruby and I bonded completely for nine months, until she was adopted by someone. We were crying as soon as we realized that she would be leaving us. So a few months after Ruby left for her new home, we adopted Edgar, intending to keep him forever but he ended up getting sick. After he passed, we adopted Grover, who's still a puppy.

So many dogs need rescuing and this is what we can do. It is incredibly rewarding and even with the pain of losing Ruby to a new owner and Edgar's death, we've never regretted taking in these dogs.

Having a dog changed us as a couple. It gave us a common goal and something to care about. It allowed us to have this extra bond; we discussed and debated what we had to do for dog. We talked more and we spent more time together, taking walks with the dog and interacting with each other, instead of going out to do our errands separately. We choose to spend this time together and take the dogs everywhere. We don't miss out on anything and the dogs have enriched our lives.

If you're interested in fostering a dog, consider these reputable organizations, The Last Resort and Rescue Haven.

—Mike Onorato

Journey to Forgiveness

I was born in Idaho at the tail end of the Depression era, to a farm girl who married a carpenter. This was a time when women typically didn't have a voice. As I grew into adulthood, I began to identify with the era of feminism. As a young wife and mother in the 1970s, I began to feel trapped and depressed. In an attempt to figure out why, an inner voice called to me. Desperate, I answered the summons, which wrenched me from my husband of fourteen years and my three young children.

Loosed from my family, severed from the life I had known for over thirty years, I felt both liberated and lost—exhilarated yet completely rudderless. With no developmental chart for starting over, I lurched forward. For a long time, I was consumed with guilt and shame, but I continued to put one foot in front of the other. Forty years later I wrote my memoir, *Flight Instructions: A Journey Through Guilt to Forgiveness*, seeking forgiveness and hoping to sweep away the last remaining crumbs of guilt. My daughters and husband had long ago forgiven me, but it took me all these decades before I could finally forgive myself.

My memoir, the telling of my story, went beyond forgiveness. It was a voyage of self-discovery, a story of triumph over demons. What began with me leaving turned into the unification of a family, of love, and healing. In spite of the early demons, I doggedly forged on, pursuing and then accomplishing amazing goals.

I joined the U.S. Army, using the G.I. Bill to support an educational pathway. I eventually earned four degrees: a bachelor's, two masters', and a Ph.D. I segued from my Ph.D. program and studied at the London School of Economics and Political Science and then joined the faculty at Louisiana State University, School of Social Work, in Baton Rouge.

The powerful spiritual dimension that I uncovered on my forty-year journey forced me to take my hands from my eyes and the shield from my heart. For much of that time I felt lost and alone, but what I now know is that there was a Higher Presence in my life as I took my *flight*. I now think of myself of especially watched over by that Presence, by God. One of my spiritual teachers said that we must listen with our hearts for the heart always speaks to us about things we cannot see; the Invisible wanting to make itself visible. I've blossomed full-orb into the true authentic person I was meant to be, into my true spiritual power.

Writing certain scenes in the memoir was painful, especially when digging up certain things from the past about leaving my children. I would experience physical pain, become ill, and would have to stop writing for a while. The symptoms were always about guilt, fear, pain, unresolved issues, loss of power, out of balance, over and over again. I could feel it in my solar plexus, then in my stomach, my back and neck, different parts in the right and left sides of my body, as well as bouts with vertigo. This was good for me, a catharsis of sorts, part of the necessary process of moving forward to forgiveness.

Although I left, I did not abandon my children. We remained in contact and saw one another with increasing frequency over the years. The book's moving epilogue brings the reader full circle as daughters and mother gather to talk, laugh, and cry as they discuss "the leaving event," its impact on their lives, and how it helped forge the girls into the strong and stalwart women they are today.

In my book, after this time together with the girls, I write a brief summary of that experience. Here are the last two sentences of that summary and of the book:

"I look at them and observe three dynamic human beings— compassionate, caring, and humane—and what I see and hear comes from a higher cosmic plane. I had a part to play in their evolution. How can I possibly feel guilty about that?"

My legacy to my daughters is a new model. My journey was not about feminist rebellion, but about a woman bringing three daughters into the world, then having to leave them to find her way back to mothering in a new, albeit nontraditional, way. As God would have it, I married the right man to father our daughters and keep them safe. Not by choice, he let me go to take the journey I came here to embark upon.

I did not start out writing about my journey to forgiveness for publication; however, after some friends and my daughters read it, they encouraged me to go public with my story. I listened to them. My hope is that those who read *Flight Instructions* will come to understand the power of forgiveness. Forgiveness does not come in an "aha" moment, it is a process. I am grateful for this process. I was able to break down the barriers to love. I'm also grateful to the players in my life who were the catalyst for my metamorphosis: my three beautiful daughters, their father, and Barbara, their stepmother, those I left behind as I set out on my journey.

As a woman coming of age in the '70s, I chose the road less traveled. I bucked up against societal norms. Some would say I had a choice. Did I? There is a long-held axiom that we all have choice. I question that, especially when it comes to matters of the heart and the soul. The mores surrounding growth and stagnation were more prominent in the '70s with specified, traditional roles for men and women. I'm not mocking this, I bought into it. I lived it. It took almost half a century for me take that sharp turn away from fear and into love and forgiveness; my spiritual birth right—my true authentic self.

My "happy ending" remains unfinished. I've discovered that forgiveness is the gift that goes on giving. The powerful mystery of life continues.

I've answered another calling, to be in service, a way of giving back. I've developed two writing workshops: "The Write Remedy: Healing Through Writing," and "The Power of Forgiveness: Writing to Heal." Both are spiritually based, interactive workshops that introduce participants to writing as a therapeutic tool serving as an effective outlet for expressing thoughts and feelings related to emotionally challenging experiences as we go from guilt/pain/shame to forgiveness. Forgiveness is at the root of a vibrant life. *Forgiveness opens the heart to love.*

—**Kathleen P. Perkins**, kathleenperkinsphd.com

The Open Hearts Foundation

If your heart is open, love will always find its way in.
—**Jane Seymour**, Open Hearts Foundation

The Open Hearts Foundation is a social impact accelerator that is committed to empowering emerging and growing nonprofit organizations, whose origins and mission are consistent with the precepts of the Open Hearts philosophy. The Foundation, by providing expertise, resources, and tools, enables these nonprofits not only to raise their profile but also further their mission and objectives.

The Open Hearts Award honors individuals who have risen above their own life challenges to truly help and reach out to others in need. The award is based on the "open heart" philosophy of founder Jane Seymour's mother, Mieke Frankenberg. Mieke moved past her own horrific experience as a World War II internment camp survivor and dedicated her life to helping others cope with adversity. The Open Hearts Award recipients have dedicated significant time and resources to nonprofits that receive grants from the Open Hearts Foundation.

For more information on Open Hearts Foundation, go to openheartsfoundation.org.

About the Author

A multiple Emmy® and Golden Globe® winner, recipient of the Officer of the British Empire (OBE) in the year 2000, which was bestowed upon her by Queen Elizabeth II at Buckingham Palace, Jane Seymour has proven her talents in virtually all media, the Broadway stage, motion pictures and television. Her love of art and color has led to her great success as a painter in watercolors and oils, as a sculptor and as a designer.

Seymour's past films include the James Bond movie *Live and Let Die,* the cult classic *Somewhere in Time,* and the comedy smash *Wedding Crashers.* Her television credits include the Emmy® Award Winning performance in *Onassis: The Richest Man in the World* as Maria Callas, *East of Eden* for which she was awarded a Golden Globe®, the mini-series *War and Remembrance* and her Golden Globe® winning role as "Dr. Quinn" on *Dr. Quinn, Medicine Woman* which ran for six seasons.

In addition to acting, Seymour has written over a dozen books, including *The Wave, Open Hearts Family, Among Angels, Open Hearts, Making Yourself At Home,* and *Remarkable Changes.*

When she is not acting or writing, Seymour can be found in her painting studio. An accomplished fine artist, her art serves as inspiration for Open Hearts by Jane Seymour®, a jewelry line she designs for KAY® Jewelers in the U.S., Peoples in Canada and H. Samuel in the U.K. Seymour's Open Heart philosophy reflects her mother's philosophy.